Invincible Christianity

Also by Dr. Steven Brooks

Working With Angels

Standing on the Shoulders of Giants

The Sacred Anointing

Fasting and Prayer

How To Operate in the Gifts of the Spirit

Manifesting the Blessings of God

Supernatural Fragrance

Invincible Christianity

Books are available in EBOOK and AUDIO BOOK through your favorite online book retailer or by request from your local bookstore.

Invincible Christianity

Empowered by the Word, Transformed by the Spirit

Dr. Steven Brooks

Rise UP
PUBLICATIONS

June 2025
ISBN: 978-1-64457-794-3 (pb)
ISBN: 978-1-64457-795-0 (hc)

Rise UP Publications
644 Shrewsbury Commons Ave
Ste 249
Shrewsbury PA 17361
United States of America
www.riseUPpublications.com
Phone: 866-846-5123

What Leading Theologians Are Saying:

"Through his writing, Pastor Steven transmits no less than his very life. It is sacred—a holy impartation. As you open this book, approach it with reverence and a heart overflowing with thanksgiving to the Lord for such an extraordinary gift—a living gift to the body of Christ."

~Father Geoffroy de Lestrange, Hermit Monk and Benedictine Parish Priest of 40 Years, Cerdon, France.

* * *

"This powerful volume is victory-based living made clear and simple. With scriptural authority and spiritual insight, believers will be speaking out their destiny to the amazement of this dark world. For those in my tradition, Pastor Steven embodies the spirit of St. Padre Pio, whose gifts have inspired us for decades. How lovely that God is uniting us all in fidelity, faith, and power!"

~Rev. Dr. Ronald Thomas, Ph. D. University of Cambridge in England, Associate Professor, Canonical Mandatum from the Diocese of Charlotte, Theology.

Dr. Steven Brooks, already a prolific author, presents his latest book, *Invincible Christianity,* where he turns the reader's attention to the essential Christian balance between the Word of God and the anointing of the Holy Spirit. His writing will give you many articulate, concise statements, which require a pause to contemplate the truths contained therein, much like the *Selah* pauses in the book of Psalms.

Dr. Brooks establishes a solid foundation of faith in God's word for his Christian readers, which will bring them into a bold position to make prophetic proclamations about God's promises concerning their lives that will indeed come to pass. This is due to having one's heart filled with faith and the words proclaimed being fully anointed by the Holy Spirit.

This book is a must-read for every sincere Christian.

~Rev. Dr. Douglas J. Wingate, Ph. D, D. Min, DD, MA, BA. Founder and President of Life Christian University. Tampa, FL.

Contents

Introduction

This book, at its heart, is two books in one. The first four chapters explore the power of the Holy Spirit, while the remaining chapters focus on the power of God's Word. When we find the right balance between the Word and the Spirit, we enter a powerful spiritual state, one where we become resilient—even invincible—against any attack from the enemy.

Sports science demonstrates that imbalances in muscle groups are a primary cause of injuries. Take the legs, for example: if the quadriceps are well-developed but the hamstrings are neglected, the body is primed for trouble. Under intense strain, the weakness in the hamstrings creates a point of vulnerability. When pushed to the limit, it's often the underdeveloped muscle group—in this case, the hamstrings—that sustains the injury. This principle underscores the importance of balanced training to build strength and resilience across all muscle groups, ensuring they work in harmony to support and protect the body during physical challenges.

In the same way, a spiritual imbalance can create its own set of challenges. Too much emphasis on the Word may cause us to become rigid, dry, and overly intellectual, while too much focus on the Spirit without the foundation of the Word can lead to emotionalism or instability.

For instance, you may find yourself in a time of revival, experiencing the Spirit's gifts in abundance—healing, deliverance, and great blessings. Yet you may still struggle in other areas, such as finances because the Word's grounding truth isn't as deeply rooted in your life as it needs to be. This is why we need the foundation of God's Word. Miracles are powerful, but we are not meant to live by miracles alone. We are called to walk by faith, and faith is nourished by the Word, which equips us to live victoriously in every circumstance.

Conversely, emphasizing the Word without the Spirit can lead to intellectualism—a form of knowledge that understands principles but lacks connection with the force of God that brings those principles to life. True beauty, both physical and spiritual, lies in symmetry. A front view may be beautiful, but if the back is undeveloped, the overall beauty is incomplete. Likewise, elegance at the top is marred if the base is disproportionate. Beauty arises from balance—when we are well-developed in both the Word and the Spirit.

In writing this book, I have sought to convey this delicate balance. As you read, meditate on, and apply these teachings, you will begin to see a shield of protection—an *invincibility* against harm—forming around your life. Each day, as you pursue God's plan, He will guide you, helping you to overcome past setbacks and any current frustrations. You will rise to prominence in your field, fulfill your divine calling, and transform into the person God designed you to be, reflecting the image of His Son, Jesus.

May God bless you abundantly on this journey of growth and transformation.

Dr. Steven Brooks

Chapter One

Tongues of Liquid Fire: Exploring the Benefits of Praying in Tongues

When talking about the Holy Spirit and the fire of the Holy Spirit, I believe God will meet you and touch you right where you are. As we study the Word of God, the Holy Spirit will quicken you so that it becomes spiritual food that you can consume and be strengthened by. There are many reasons you should pray in tongues and walk with God in the Holy Spirit, drawing closer to the Lord.

> Knowing this first, that no prophecy of Scripture is of any private interpretation, for prophecy never came by the will of man, but holy men of God spoke as they were moved by the Holy Spirit.
>
> — 2 Peter 1:20-21

The Holy Spirit is the author of the Old and the New Testaments. All sixty-six books were written by men of God as the Holy Spirit inspired them to write God's message. All of these books were put together as one complete book, known as the Bible. But here's something interesting: To rightly interpret God's Word, we need to rely on the Holy Spirit to reveal what He meant when these men wrote these books and letters. There are some scriptures that are very challenging to interpret. The Holy Spirit was sent to us in Jesus' place. The Holy Spirit is the person who inspired the scriptures we rely on. He knows all depths of scriptural meanings. A closeness with the Holy Spirit can provide accurate understanding and revelation of God's Word.

There are additional scriptures, especially those dealing with eschatology, that provide some insight into this particular subject. While we might wish for more detailed explanations in certain areas, it's clear that God didn't consider it essential; otherwise, He would have included more scriptures on the topic. Eschatology, which explores the sequence of end-time events, is indeed a captivating study, but it's crucial to approach it with the Holy Spirit's guidance. Without His help, we risk relying too heavily on our intellect alone, which is insufficient for grasping the full depth of these divine revelations.

As you draw nearer to the Holy Spirit through speaking in tongues, you will gain supernatural insight into the deeper meaning of Scripture. You'll begin to see the contrast between those who have intellectual ability only, and those who utilize their minds to the highest degree while also connecting with and trusting the Holy Spirit for enlightenment.

In the fourth chapter of the Book of Ephesians, I want to point out that Jesus is the originator of your own unique individual callings. That calling could be ministry, business, or sales. It could be a career in the medical field, but whatever it might be, Jesus is the originator of your own unique calling.

Here's a great example:

> He who descended is also the One who ascended far above all the heavens, that He might fill all things. And He Himself gave some to be apostles, some prophets, some evangelists, and some pastors and teachers.
>
> — Ephesians 4:10-11

We see here that Jesus is the originator of giving out the individual callings for ministers and their respected offices, but it's important that we know that it is the Holy Spirit who reveals and sets us into those callings. This is amazing.

> From Miletus he sent to Ephesus and called for the elders of the church.
>
> — Acts 20:17

Paul sent to Ephesus and called for the elders of the church, and when they came to him, he began to talk about some things.

> Therefore take heed to yourselves and to all the flock, among which the Holy Spirit has made you overseers, to shepherd the church of God which He purchased with His own blood.
>
> — Acts 20:28

The Holy Spirit made them overseers. Jesus is the one who is the originator of the calling, but the Holy Spirit is the one who releases the supernatural equipment that goes along with that office or with that calling, and that's what makes all the difference in the world. Praise God.

Another example that displays the ministry of the Holy Spirit:

> Now in the church that was at Antioch there were certain prophets and teachers: Barnabas, Simeon who was called Niger, Lucius of Cyrene, Manaen who had been brought up with Herod the tetrarch, and Saul. As they ministered to the Lord and fasted, the Holy Spirit said, "Now separate to Me Barnabas and Saul for the work to which I have called them."
>
> — Acts 13:1-2

The Holy Spirit placed them into those positions that Jesus had destined for them to walk in, and He will do the same for you. *"Then having fasted and prayed and laid hands on them they sent them away, being sent out by the Holy Spirit"* (Acts 13:3). It makes a huge difference whether you send yourself or the Holy Spirit sends you. They're sent out into the apostolic ministry, which is what Jesus had prepared for them. The Holy Spirit is not only empowering them, setting them into those positions, but *timing is also very important* because before they were released into the apostolic ministry, we see them serving as teachers, some as prophets, and I'm sure some as both teachers and prophets.

Timing is critical. We must rely upon the Holy Spirit for the empowering, the sending, and the timing of when to go. It is important to realize that the Holy Spirit is the one who controls your destiny. Jesus has your destiny in His hand. Jesus has the plan and purpose, but the Holy Spirit has so much to do with the fulfillment of it and the walking out of it in your life.

Understanding the role of the Holy Spirit leads us naturally into the supernatural phenomenon of speaking in tongues. When you speak in tongues, which is synonymous with praying in the Holy Spirit, you gain insight into God's plan and purpose for your life. Whether that plan involves stepping into an apostolic ministry, like Paul, who was sent out and ended up traveling across the Middle East and Europe preaching the Gospel, or whether it's God calling you into business, media, or another field, praying in tongues allows the Holy Spirit to guide you into the destiny that Jesus ordained for you before you were even born. Glory to God.

> And it happened, while Apollos was at Corinth, that Paul, having passed through the upper regions, came to Ephesus. And finding some disciples he said to them, "Did you receive the Holy Spirit when you believed?"
> So they said to him, "We have not so much as heard whether there is a Holy Spirit."
> And he said to them, "Into what then were you baptized?"
> So they said, "Into John's baptism."
>
> — Acts 19:1-3

> When they heard this, they were baptized in the name of the Lord Jesus. And when Paul had laid hands on them, the Holy Spirit came upon them, and they spoke with

> tongues and prophesied. Now the men were about twelve in all.
>
> — Acts 19:5-7

These twelve men were believers and had even been water baptized, but they had not yet been filled with the Spirit, evidenced by speaking in other tongues. This passage clearly shows a distinction between the first step, which is the salvation experience where you're born again, and the Holy Spirit comes to live within you by measure, and the subsequent experience of being filled with the Holy Spirit to overflow. When you receive this infilling of the Holy Spirit, you also receive your new prayer language, which is speaking in tongues.

Speaking in tongues is the evidence that you have received the infilling of the Holy Spirit. To clarify, a believer must first confess their faith in the Lord Jesus Christ. After salvation, it is necessary to follow the Lord's instructions and be baptized in water. At this point, a born-again believer can receive the baptism in the Holy Spirit. There's the initial infilling, but then, there can also be a fresh filling or a *topping off* with new oil.

When you get saved, you can be filled with the Spirit, and even after that, you can receive a fresh infilling. It's like maintaining a vehicle. My vehicle, for instance, holds six quarts of oil, which is standard for a V8 engine. But every 3,000 miles, I get the oil changed. All six quarts of dirty, black oil are drained out because clean oil is essential for the smooth operation of the engine.

Scripture tells us, *"All His works are numerous"* (Psalm 104:24), meaning everything in our lives works together, and one area can affect another. The Holy Spirit will show you which areas of your life may need attention to ensure the multi-faceted design of your life functions smoothly. Now, imagine if you only drained out four quarts of dirty oil but left two quarts of that black, contaminated oil in your engine, and then added fresh oil. That's not what the manufacturer intended for optimum performance, and in the same way, God desires for your life to operate at its peak potential.

When you pray in tongues, when you pray in the Spirit, you experience that needed oil change, where all the impurities and contaminants are flushed out, and you are refilled with brand-new oil. This process cleanses all the sludge, even from the deepest parts of your soul, ensuring a thorough cleansing by the Holy Spirit.

The Apostle Paul gives us further insight into speaking in tongues:

> For if I pray in a tongue, my spirit prays, but my understanding is unfruitful.
>
> — 1 Corinthians 14:14

The Holy Spirit doesn't do the praying for you; He provides the utterance. As you fellowship with the Holy Spirit and commune with God, your spirit speaks the utterance that the Holy Spirit provides.

You are a spirit, and you have a soul. Your soul comprises your mind, will, and emotions. You live in a body. Just as we can develop our minds and bodies—which is essential for maturity in the natural realm—we must also develop our inner man. Praying in tongues, or praying in the Holy Spirit, is the key to maturing your spirit and deepening your walk with the Lord. Just as you learned to read as a child and improved your reading skills over time with practice, you can expand your ability to discern where the Holy Spirit is leading you through consistent practice of speaking in tongues. This spiritual discipline will guide you toward the destiny path and eventual fulfillment that the Lord has planned for you.

The prophet Isaiah said this in the Book of Isaiah:

> For with stammering lips and another tongue He will speak
> to this people, To whom He said, "This is the rest with
> which You may cause the weary to rest," And,
> "This is the refreshing"; Yet they would not hear.
>
> — Isaiah 28:11-12

Notice the emphasis on rest: *"This is the rest with which You may cause the weary to rest, and this is the refreshing."* Speaking in tongues brings rest to the weary and a divine refreshing.

Let's now look again at 1 Corinthians, a book that contains the most comprehensive teachings in the Bible on the subject of tongues and the interpretation of tongues:

> In the law it is written:
> "With men of other tongues and other lips I will speak to
> this people; And yet, for all that, they will not hear Me,"
> says the Lord.
>
> — 1 Corinthians 14:21

In this verse, Paul is quoting from Isaiah 28:11-12, referencing what we now know in the New Covenant as speaking in tongues.

Isaiah said it would produce rest: *"For with stammering lips and another tongue He will speak to this people, to whom He said, 'This is the rest with which You may cause the weary to rest,' and, 'This is the refreshing....'"*

This is why you should desire it—why you need it—because speaking in tongues brings a supernatural rest and an unexplainable refreshing. I can personally testify that it indeed brings rest and refreshing into your life, something much needed in today's world. We hear about wars, terrible events, and hideous acts committed against innocent people. We are living in a time where gross darkness is often displayed before us. Yet, even in this world, we can walk in rest and refreshing because we pray often in tongues.

It's becoming increasingly evident that world leaders lack the answers and solutions to the problems their countries face. The Church, however, has the answers because the challenges are common to all men, and these various needs are all addressed and resolved through the wisdom of God's Word. Through the rest and refreshing that come from the Holy Spirit, the Church will present a sharp contrast to the anxiety of the world, drawing many people to Jesus.

Speaking in tongues causes the river of God to flow through you, bringing refreshing and rest in the Lord. Look at what Jesus said:

> On the last day, that great day of the feast, Jesus stood and cried out, saying, "If anyone thirsts, let him come to Me and drink. He who believes in Me, as the Scripture has said, out of his heart will flow rivers of living water." But this He spoke concerning the Spirit, whom those believing in Him would receive; for the Holy

> Spirit was not yet given, because Jesus was not yet glorified.
>
> —John 7:37-39

The heart often refers to the spirit of man, so you could say, out of your spirit, or out of your heart, will flow rivers of living water. *"But this He spoke concerning the Spirit, whom those believing in Him would receive; for the Holy Spirit was not yet given, because Jesus was not yet glorified."*

Jesus announced this before His crucifixion, but we know He has since been glorified, raised from the dead, ascended into Heaven, and is now seated at the right hand of God. The Holy Spirit was poured out upon those in the Upper Room, and He is still being poured out upon God's people today.

When you speak in tongues, when you pray in the Spirit, living waters by the Spirit of God begin to flow out of you, bringing rest and refreshing. You can immerse yourself in that river and experience profound peace and joy.

Here are some of the many fascinating benefits of praying in tongues:

Speaking in tongues brings rest and refreshing, and a river of living water flows from your heart and your spirit. It represents unstoppable progress against any dark force that tries to oppose your life. Tongues also builds and stimulates your faith because every time you open your mouth to speak in tongues, it requires faith.

Tongues empower you to break free from wrong thinking patterns. When I first began speaking in tongues, I was still influenced by religious tradition, which had shaped my mentality through years of misinformation and incorrect teachings. As a young boy growing up, we attended church every Sunday morning, Sunday night, and Wednesday night.

I'm grateful to my mom and dad for taking me and my brothers to church, but along with that, we absorbed a lot of religious tradition, not biblical tradition, but religious tradition. Speaking in tongues was preached against, and the supernatural was strongly opposed. We were warned that speaking in tongues and modern-day miracles were of the devil and were cautioned to stay away from it.

So, when I discovered that God's power was real and that you could be filled with the Spirit and speak in tongues, I knew from Scripture that it was a valid experience for today. However, my mind was still gripped by fear due to all the fallacies and wrong information I had received.

The first time I spoke in tongues, I started slowly, but soon it began to flow faster and faster. As the words rolled out of me, picking up speed, my mind wrestled with what was happening in my spirit. I kept speaking in tongues faster and faster, determined to override my mind. For almost three days, I focused almost entirely on speaking in tongues. Why? I wanted to wash away that old mental fortress of religious tradition from my mind. I could sense it dissolving the more time I spent praying in tongues, until it was completely washed away like a sandcastle at the beach during high tide. Today, I can speak in tongues anytime, anywhere, and it refreshes me, though it still takes faith because it's a supernatural manifestation.

Speaking in tongues serves as a catalyst for creative ideas, profitable investments, and new forms of artistic expression. When spoken softly, tongues create an atmosphere conducive to meditation and deep reflection, helping you ponder solutions to life's challenges. When spoken with strength and conviction, tongues facilitate breakthroughs and empower you to conquer the Canaan-land inheritance that God has promised you.

Speaking in tongues is your gateway into the realm of the Spirit, often referred to as the Glory Zone. When you make it a habit to regularly speak in tongues, it will encourage the activation and flow of the nine gifts of the Holy Spirit in your life.

Tongues are also a way to pray for things that are hidden so that they can be revealed. *"For he who speaks in a tongue does not speak to men but to God, for no one understands him; however, in the spirit he speaks mysteries"* (1 Corinthians 14:2). These mysteries often pertain to your destiny and divine assignment, which have been concealed to protect them from the enemy. As you pray in tongues, these secrets are gradually unveiled to your understanding.

Tongues also keep you spiritually fit, preventing you from becoming distracted or entangled in the illusions of this world. It helps stabilize you, making you keenly aware that you are seated with Christ in heavenly places, far above the noise and confusion of earthly matters.

Furthermore, speaking in tongues equips you to perceive the exquisite wonders of God through your spiritual senses—seeing, hearing, tasting, touching, and smelling in the spirit realm. It fine-tunes and calibrates your spirit man, making you increasingly sensitive to the leading of the Holy Spirit.

Speaking in tongues strengthens your inner man with might and enhances your accuracy in operating in the spiritual gifts bestowed upon you.

Speaking in tongues plays a vital role in aligning your life with God's divine plan. For example, once, during a lunch break at work, I began praying in the Spirit, and tongues flowed effortlessly for about 40 minutes. Afterward, the Holy Spirit gave me clear guidance to include a specific supernatural experience in a book manuscript I was working on—a detail I had completely forgotten. Years later, many pastors have told me how much that story impacted them. Without the Holy Spirit's prompting, it wouldn't have made it into the book. This illustrates how tongues helps you pray out God's meticulously crafted plan for your life.

Tongues also offers practical solutions to life's complex problems. Because it's a deep spiritual practice, it equips you to tackle the deep and significant challenges of life with divine insight.

Moreover, tongues is the believer's direct access to God's throne room. It's like your personal spiritual Starlink system, far more advanced than satellite internet, enabling high-speed, direct communication with God.

Beyond being a spiritual exercise, tongues is a gateway into the supernatural. It elevates your praise and thanksgiving to God beyond the limits of natural language.

Tongues cultivates a heightened awareness of God's presence, drawing you deeper into His glory. Though believers have the mind of Christ, it is through the regular practice of speaking in tongues that we fully experience this divine mind within us.

Tongues also tunes you into the realm of miracles. You start to feel an inner shift, a profound awareness that with God, nothing is impossible. This awareness manifests as a vibrant energy within—a resonance that assures you of God's active power in your life. As you engage more in speaking in tongues, genuine miracles begin to unfold, not only for you but also for those you pray for. In this way, tongues broadens your understanding of God's miraculous abilities and how they can manifest in your life.

Furthermore, tongues plays a significant role in receiving and maintaining healing. It provides spiritual refreshing and rest, similar to having around-the-clock access to your own private resort spa.

Tongues amplifies the anointing's *fatness*, which is the greasy, oily substance that lubricates the neck, destroying the yoke, as referenced in Isaiah 10:27.

Praying in tongues helps bring your natural speech under control. Among all the benefits of praying in tongues, this one stands out to me like pure gold. Let me emphasize this again: speaking in tongues assists in subduing your natural tongue. When you rise early and dedicate an hour to praying in tongues, you'll find that as you go about your day, you're less likely to say things that are out of place or inappropriate.

When a conversation veers into a situation where silence is wisest, your ability to hold your tongue becomes much easier if you've spent time in early morning prayer. Through consistent prayer in tongues, your tongue learns to come under the subjection of the Holy Spirit. On the other hand, when you're operating in the flesh, it can be difficult to resist the impulse to speak out of turn because your tongue isn't being governed by the Spirit. However, when you've been praying in tongues, a supernatural calm comes over you, allowing you to hold back and refrain from speaking. It can feel unusual because, under normal circumstances, you might have been drawn into the conversation, compelled to speak, and potentially veered off course. But something extraordinary happens when you pray in tongues: it grants you control over your speech.

Praying in tongues serves as a powerful aid in bringing your natural speech under the influence of your renewed, born-again spirit. It helps prevent you from reacting in the flesh, as the devil uses various tactics to provoke ungodly responses during moments of pressure. Tongues keeps you from falling into these traps, ensuring that the enemy cannot provoke you into a wrong reaction. I can't fully explain how this works, but I can affirm that it does work—in a strikingly supernatural way.

Speaking in tongues is like intermingling yourself with fire. Just as fire produces an immediate reaction when it touches your hand, tongues can bring about instantaneous, powerful results.

Tongues also gives you a complete spiritual oil change—not just a partial one where some of the old oil and sludge remain. Instead, it's a full system flush that cleanses and renews you entirely.

Through tongues, the Holy Spirit works inwardly to transform you. It's a process that reaches deep into your soul, uprooting character flaws and replacing them with good fruit. The very things that caused failure in your life will be put to death.

Tongues offer a private conversation with God that no one else, not even the most advanced surveillance, can understand. When you speak in your personal prayer language of tongues, the message cannot be intercepted or decoded by the enemy.

Tongues is deep calling unto deep, creating a pathway into God's presence that helps you overcome despair, as described in Psalm 42:7. It accesses revelation knowledge, tapping into the mind of God and enabling you to think and solve problems with a super-human level of intelligence.

Tongues is also a way of worshiping the Heavenly Father in Spirit and in truth. While you can certainly pray in English—and if done in alignment with God's Word, you are indeed praying in the Spirit—praying in tongues ensures that you are 100 percent in the Spirit. This means you are praying the perfect will and plan of God, without any selfish motives or wrong intentions. The Holy Spirit empowers you, praying through you, and as you speak in tongues, you are praying out God's perfect will for your life.

When you pray in tongues, it charges your spiritual battery. Just as we charge our cell phones daily, we must also charge our spirits to full capacity. Without a fully charged spirit, you won't be ready to take charge in life. Good intentions and efforts will only get you so far; you need to be fully charged to succeed.

Tongues build the likeness of God within you, instilling confidence and transforming your self-perception. No longer will you see yourself as a victim or a pushover. Instead, you will see yourself as more than a conqueror. When the enemy attacks you with fear or nightmares, you won't be paralyzed. Instead, you will rise up, fighting back with the strength of a lion, causing the enemy to flee in terror.

Tongues are one of the primary indicators mentioned by Jesus as a sign of those who belong to Him:

"And these signs will follow those who believe: In My name,

> they will cast out demons; they will speak with new tongues."
>
> — Mark 16:17

Tongues help manifest God's specific plan for your life, guiding you to discover where you fit in. They also tap into God's wisdom, helping you untangle the complex problems you face. As you pray in tongues, you build a deeper understanding of spiritual matters, allowing you to walk more confidently in God's purpose for your life.

Tongues is a dividing line within the church, distinguishing those who enjoy the power of God and those who don't. Tongues is the key gift that the devil has fought the hardest to discredit and remove from the church. Satan is fearful of Christians who draw near to God through praying in tongues.

In the following story, Pastor Dave Roberson shares insightful wisdom that reveals why the enemy hates the gift of speaking in tongues so much.

> "I know a man whose sister was in a car accident. She was transported to the hospital, her life hanging by a thread. This man was a man of faith. As he drove to the hospital as fast as he could, he repeatedly confessed, 'My sister will live and not die; she will live and not die!' But every time he made this confession, something would shatter his emotions so intensely that it shook him from the top of his head to the bottom of his feet. Then the thought would hit him: 'She'll die!' This happened again and again as he sped toward the hospital, shaking him up more and more.

> Then suddenly, through the gift of discerning of spirits, God opened the man's spiritual eyes. (The discerning of spirits allows you to see into the realm of the spirit, whether angels or demons.) When God opened his eyes, he saw two demons—one sitting on his left shoulder, the other on his right. Every time the man would confess, 'She'll live and not die,' one demon would scream through his ear to the other demon, 'She'll die! She'll die!' Then the Lord spoke to the man in his spirit: 'Make your confession, and then begin to pray in tongues.'
>
> So the man made his confession one more time and began to pray in tongues. After a while, one of the demons looked around the back of the man's head at the other demon and said, 'What do you think he's saying?' The other demon replied, 'I don't know, but is it burning you the way it's burning me?' 'Yes,' the other demon answered. 'Do you think we should leave?' So they left. And you may as well know, the man's sister lived and did not die!"[1]

Speaking in tongues is an act of praying from your spirit. It grants your eternal spirit its rightful supremacy over the lowly nature of your flesh. For many, the flesh has been a relentless taskmaster, acting like a self-entitled dictator. Perhaps you've experienced years where your flesh has ruled over you, dictating your actions and decisions. However, the moment you begin to speak in tongues, the crown of dominion starts to pass from the base and crude state of the flesh to the exalted position of your born-again, recreated spirit.

---

1. *The Walk of the Spirit – The Walk of Power: The Vital Role of Praying in Tongues* by Dave Roberson, Copyright 1999 by Dave Roberson Ministries.

Praying in tongues establishes the correct biblical order in your life, which is divinely designed by God to be *spirit, soul, and body*. It's worth noting one of the most misquoted verses in the Bible: *"Now may the God of peace Himself sanctify you completely; and may your whole spirit, soul, and body be preserved blameless at the coming of our Lord Jesus Christ"* (1 Thessalonians 5:23). Many Christians often quote this verse in reverse, saying, *"body, soul, and spirit."*

Why does this happen? It's because people are generally more aware of their bodies than their spirits. They are more conscious of their soul—their mind, will, and emotions—than of their spirit. Consequently, the spirit, which should be at the forefront, often gets the least acknowledgment. However, Paul, guided by divine revelation, stated it in the correct order: *spirit, soul, and body*.

By praying in tongues, you begin to align yourself with this divine order, allowing your spirit to take its rightful place as the leading force in your life. This spiritual alignment not only empowers your spirit but also brings your entire being—your soul and body—into harmony with God's perfect design for you.

Speaking in tongues is your human spirit communicating with your Heavenly Father in the Secret Place. In this divine exchange, God understands every word you utter in the Spirit. Tongues can be spoken, but they can also take the form of a song, expanding your ability to worship God more fully.

Speaking in tongues unleashes the refreshing winds of personal revival in your life. It leads to mentorship by the Holy Spirit, helping you crush the impure cravings of the flesh until they are as flat as a pancake run over by a steamroller. Through this process, you come to realize that you are dead to sin, having been crucified with Christ.

The most important gift the Heavenly Father gave to the world was Jesus. The most important gift Jesus gave to the Church after His departure was the Holy Spirit. The most important gift the Holy Spirit gave to the Church is your personal prayer language of speaking in tongues.

Tongues set captives free from gloomy dungeons of despair. Some forms of liberation only God can perform, especially when painful events are deeply embedded within a person's soul. Tongues play a crucial role in this divine healing process.

Praying in tongues is like consuming the fresh wine of the Holy Spirit, which, unlike alcohol, doesn't kill brain cells. Tongues allow you to explore the supernatural, venturing into uncharted territories where many have not yet sailed. They are like rocket propellants, helping you break free from the gravitational pull of the enticing but corrupt world system.

Tongues leads you into the initial phase of being led by the Holy Spirit. The more you pray in the Spirit, the more sensitive you become to the inner guidance and witness of the Holy Spirit.

Tongues enables you to please God because you cannot please Him without faith, and tongues builds up your faith.

Tongues dissipates the agitation of the flesh, allowing you to pray longer, focus more clearly, and wait more patiently in the presence of the Lord. Tongues are essential for opening your spiritual understanding to experience fresh insights from God's Word on an ongoing basis.

Speaking in tongues is a powerful spiritual weapon that causes your enemies to fall into the traps they've set for you. It empowers you to walk in your heritage as a servant of the Lord, fulfilling Isaiah

54:17: *"No weapon formed against you shall prosper, and every tongue which rises against you in judgment you shall condemn."* Through this divine language, you invoke God's intervention, ensuring the enemy's plans are defeated.

Tongues are like a *blue-sky* thinking session with God. You have the ability to sit down and conceptualize with Him concerning His plan for your life and how to accomplish it in sequential phases.

Tongues express trust and reliance on God, serving as an expression of humility. They are like drilling for the golden oil of creativity, placed deep within the core of your vast human spirit.

Tongues allow the Holy Spirit to search your heart and pray the perfect will of God through you, which will always be in complete harmony with His Word.

Tongues cultivate a calm boldness in your speech—a quality of leadership born from inner strength. They align you seamlessly with the prophetic timing of God, helping you recognize kairos moments that bring opportunities for ministry, divine connections, and financial increase.

Tongues carry you into the poetic expressions of the Spirit, transforming you into a pun-dropping, fun-loving enigma. They open the Word of God to you with revelatory knowledge, just as they did for Saint Paul the Apostle. Paul's revelations were as powerful as those Moses received on Mount Sinai when God gave Israel the Law. His source of revelatory knowledge stemmed from extensive speaking and praying in tongues.

Tongues send angels on heavenly assignments to perform the will of God. When you're praying in tongues, you're communicating with God. However, there are times when your prayer language shifts, and the Holy Spirit causes you to issue declarations and instructions to angels. These angels then go out on assignment, fulfilling those instructions and rendering aid to those in need—often without your conscious awareness of what is taking place.

In chapter one of the book *War Beyond the Stars* by Joel and Jane French, the author shared an insightful testimony:

> A Jewish rabbi went to visit a pastor friend in Pasadena, California. The rabbi had been saved and baptized in the Holy Spirit and was to share his testimony with a local Christian businesswoman's chapter that met for lunch. Before going to the lunch meeting, the pastor gave the rabbi a tour of his church; it was during the time of the men's morning prayer meeting. When they came to the prayer room, they passed quietly without disturbing the men who were praying. As they passed by the door of the room, one of the men began praying loudly in his heavenly language. The pastor moved on as he was accustomed to this kind of prayer. However, the rabbi lingered at the door.
>
> After a short while, the pastor approached the rabbi and told him that it was time to leave, reminding him of the speaking engagement at the upcoming luncheon. But the rabbi placed his finger across his lips and motioned for the pastor not to talk. The rabbi listened to the man who continued to pray, while the pastor waited impatiently. After a while, there was silence. The rabbi inquired, "Who was that man praying? What languages does he know?" The pastor replied, "He is an uneducated man here in the church. He knows no languages other than English. I know him well. I will introduce you to him so that you can verify for yourself."

> Then the rabbi described to the pastor that he had just listened to the most beautiful and perfect Hebrew that he had ever heard spoken. He said the man had been speaking praises to God in psalms in *English blank verse* for about fifteen to twenty minutes. Blank verse is the name given to poetry that lacks rhymes but *does* follow a specific meter. Blank verse was particularly popular in English poetry written between the 16th and 20th centuries, including the plays of Shakespeare.
> Excitedly, he said, "But the most amazing thing then happened: Still speaking in perfect Hebrew, the man switched from the psalms and began calling angels by name and sending them on missions. Angels were called by their Hebrew names and were sent on specific missions to aid those who needed help. Some were sent to aid missionaries in trouble, and the name and location of the missionary were also mentioned in the Hebrew language."[2] The rabbi was left visibly shaken by this miraculous sign.

I've also read and studied extensively about the ministry of Padre Pio (1887-1968), the Catholic Capuchin priest and monk. He was well-versed in the area of working with angels. Father Alessio, who was at Padre Pio's side for six years, states:

> "I clearly understand how many people sent their Guardian Angels to him when they wished him to receive some message or to be remembered in his prayers. In fact, passing through the crowd with him, as I did every day, I often heard it said: 'Father, as I will not be able to come to see you again,

2. *War Beyond the Stars* by Joel and Jane French, Copyright 1979. New Leaf Press

> what should I do if I need your prayers?' And Padre Pio would reply, 'If you cannot come to me, send me your Guardian Angel. He can take a message from you to me, and I will assist you as much as I can.'"[3]

Father Alessio describes how a continuous procession of angels was sent to Padre Pio throughout the day, especially at night. Padre Pio, a spiritual father to countless sons and daughters around the world, was seen as their pastor and mentor. It's no wonder he scarcely slept, as the angels brought him prayer requests from those who trusted in his grace to intercede with God. Operating in the prophetic ministry office, Padre Pio possessed the public usage gifts of tongues and interpretation of tongues. He only spoke Italian and Latin, but these gifts enabled him to communicate effortlessly with countless foreigners in the confessional despite not knowing their languages.

---

3. *"Send Me Your Guardian Angel", Padre Pio* by Father Alessio Parente, Order Of Friars Minor, Capuchin. Copyright 1983. Page 86-90. padrepio.org

Chapter Two

What Happened When I Prayed in Tongues for Fifteen Hours

When you pray in tongues often, you begin to receive insights about God's plan for your life. In my mid-20s, while I was still single, I spent a lot of time in prayer and began to sense that God had a destiny for me that involved living in Southern California. At that time, I was living in Texas, but I found myself increasingly drawn to Southern California. I even began going to the library to study books about the region. As I prayed about this, I felt a growing inner conviction that, eventually, I would live there.

However, being young in the Lord and relatively new to the Pentecostal experience, I lacked the maturity to understand the importance of God's timing. In my immaturity, I decided to just pack up and move to Southern California.

At the time, I was renting a small efficiency unit behind my pastor's house. I was so determined to move that I didn't even inform my pastor of my plans. I packed my car with all my belongings—a process that didn't take long, as I didn't own much. My plan was to attend the church service the next morning, sing in the choir as usual, enjoy the sermon, and then, as soon as the service was over, get in my car and drive straight to Southern California—despite having no idea which specific city I would go to.

I went to sleep Saturday night with my car packed and ready to go. On Sunday morning, I arrived at the church early, as I always did, to assist one of the deacons with preparations for the service. When I pulled into the church parking lot and stepped out of my car, I looked toward the entrance doors. At that moment, the double doors swung open and out walked Sister Dorothy, a deeply dedicated Christian and a powerful woman of prayer.

She stood on the steps of the church, pointed her finger with authority, and said, "Brother Brooks, I don't know what you're about to do, but God told me to tell you—don't do it. You kept me up all night praying for you." Then she turned around, muttering something about the timing of what I wanted to do being wrong, and walked back into the church.

This encounter shocked me and left me somewhat discouraged. After the service, I went home and unpacked everything. Life returned to normal for another two years. During that time, I immersed myself in reading and studying the Bible, Christian books, and anything I could find to strengthen my knowledge of God. I also secured a wonderful job with a reputable company that had been in business for over 80 years, with multiple offices in various states. I had a promising career path ahead of me and even had my own office. It was the best-paying job I ever had.

Each morning before work, I would rise early to pray and prepare for the day. My prayer time always began promptly at 6 a.m. As usual, I got out of bed one morning, went to my prayer area, and knelt down to pray. The moment I did, the Holy Spirit swept over me like a wave, speaking to me with a clear and authoritative voice: "Leave immediately and go to California."

Hearing this, I felt a twinge of concern. My previous failed attempt to move to California two years earlier had left me apprehensive. Despite the clarity with which the Holy Spirit spoke, I tried to ignore the instruction and continued praying. However, at exactly 6:10 a.m., the Holy Spirit again swept over me like a wave, repeating the command: "Leave immediately and go to California."

Faith comes from hearing the word of God. Whenever God talks, it is the release of light, the release of understanding. Whenever the will of God is revealed, then faith is always standing there, ready to go to work to accomplish what God said. I couldn't deny that I had heard from God. I stopped praying, got up, and began packing everything I owned into my car. After getting dressed, I drove to my job to inform my boss of what was happening.

When I arrived at the factory, I stepped out of my car, dressed in comfortable clothes rather than my work attire, knowing I'd be driving all day. My boss, John, saw me and called out, "Hey Steven, what's going on?" I replied, "John, I need to talk with you." He invited me into his office—a spacious room with a beautiful mahogany desk and a luxurious leather chair, a setting that felt a bit intimidating.

As we sat down, John asked, "So Steven, tell me what's going on." I hesitated, then said, "John, I don't know how to explain this to you." He responded, "Just go ahead and say it." Taking a deep breath, I explained, "This morning, at 6 o'clock, the Holy Spirit told me to leave immediately and go to California."

John raised his hand, signaling for me to stop. He reached into a drawer in his desk and pulled out a bottle of olive oil. Unscrewing the lid, he walked around the desk to where I was sitting, poured the oil on my head, and pointed at me, saying, "Go." He added, "I'll mail your final check when you get there. Just send me your new address once you know it."

He then asked, "Where in California are you going?" I replied, "I'm not entirely sure; I'm just heading in that direction." He nodded thoughtfully, and I walked out of the office. Much later, I learned that John was part of a Spirit-filled businessmen's fellowship, so he was well-versed in the workings of the Spirit.

Determined to keep my faith strong, I decided that since I was embarking on something I had never done before, I would pray in tongues all the way from Texas to Southern California. And so, I began my journey—driving, drinking water, and praying in tongues as I went.

Praying in tongues brought me a profound sense of calm, especially since I had never undertaken anything like this before. My mind was naturally concerned, but the more I prayed in the Spirit, the more I sensed a soothing comfort washing over me, dispelling any anxiety or fear. As the hours passed by on the road, the enemy frequently whispered doubts, suggesting that my car—a 24-year-old vehicle with bald tires and numerous mechanical issues—would inevitably break down. Yet, I kept praying in the Spirit and pressed on.

After 14 hours of driving and praying in tongues, I reached the mountains of New Mexico. Feeling a bit physically exhausted, I rolled down the window, allowing the cool, fresh air to keep me awake and alert. I drove for another hour, reaching the midnight hour. By this time, I had been praying in tongues non-stop for 15 hours. Suddenly, I felt a surge of energy from the Holy Spirit—an overwhelming power, unlike anything I had ever experienced before.

Tongues began to pour out of me at a faster and deeper level, like liquid fire. The only word I could use to describe it would be *ferocious*. I began praying with an intensity that made me feel like a man from another world, as if I was engaged in some intense spiritual warfare. It was clear that the Holy Spirit was praying through me, expressing the 100 percent perfect will of God. His power flowed through me like molten lava, and I thought to myself, *"Lord, I don't know how much longer I can sustain this."*

The intensity was so overwhelming that I felt as if I might explode if it continued any longer. But then, just as suddenly, the intensity broke, and a wave of heavenly peace washed over me. I looked out the window at the clear night sky, seeing the moon and stars, and in that exact moment, I witnessed something extraordinary.

I saw an evil principality falling from the sky, on fire, like a meteor. It was unmistakably a demonic prince with bat-like wings, tumbling as it was cast down from the second Heaven in the upper atmosphere to the Earth. It reminded me of when Jesus said He saw Satan fall like lightning. The Lord revealed to me that this was an evil principality assigned by Satan to derail my destiny, to prevent the ministry and calling that God had placed on my life from ever coming to fruition.

But through the power of the Holy Spirit, that principality had been defeated. The victory was clear—God's plan for my life would not be thwarted.

After this dramatic encounter with the power of God, I pulled over and slept for about six hours before continuing my journey the next day.

Something else remarkable happened during the trip as well. For years, I had struggled with extremely poor eyesight, which seemed to worsen with each passing day. My glasses were abnormally thick—so much so that it was a wonder I could even see through them. Without them, I was nearly legally blind, especially at night, which was both embarrassing and deeply frustrating. I couldn't read a single sign in the dark without my glasses, and this condition disturbed me so much that I decided to focus my faith on receiving healing for my eyes. For about two years, I consistently confessed each day that I had *Hawkeye vision,* affirming that my eyesight was exceptional. I held firmly to the words of Jesus in Mark 11:23, believing that I could have what I said, using that as the foundation for receiving my healing.

On that drive to California, I had my glasses on the entire time. However, when I finally reached the state, I decided to take a break at a welcome rest area. Having driven since early morning, I needed a moment to refresh. After stopping, I freshened up in the restroom, then returned to my car and sat on the hood to relax. Without thinking, I took off my glasses, placed them on the hood, and massaged my eyes, taking in a few deep breaths. Feeling renewed, I got back in the car and merged onto the interstate, continuing my journey.

About ten minutes later, I suddenly realized—*where were my glasses?* It hit me that I had left them on the hood of my car. By now, they were surely long gone, blown off somewhere on the side of the road. There was no turning back. I thought to myself,

"Lord, I'm going to have to trust You for the healing I've been believing for."

After arriving in Southern California and getting settled, I knew I needed to get a new driver's license. I went to the California DMV, passed the written test, and then it was time for the eye exam. For the first time in years, I would be taking this test without my glasses. Yet, I sensed that God had done something miraculous in my eyes.

Standing behind the line, I read off every letter and number on the chart perfectly. The DMV clerk told me I had passed, but I was enjoying this newfound clarity so much that I stepped further back and read an even smaller print. She commented that I had gotten those right as well, but I had already passed the test. I explained that I was just doing it for personal enjoyment, stepping back even further to read the smallest line on the chart. Again, I got them all right.

For about a full year, I walked in a realm where my eyesight was beyond 20/20. That was over thirty years ago, and while my vision isn't as strong as it used to be, it's nowhere near as poor as it once was. I do wear glasses today, but only when driving or ministering. Sometimes, I think about refocusing my faith to walk in that realm of *Hawkeye vision* once more, but I remain forever grateful that I'm no longer in the place where my eyesight was so weak.

Without a doubt, speaking in tongues for that extended period played a crucial role in strengthening my faith to receive the healing I needed for my eyes. Over the years, I have received countless emails from believers who experienced physical healing after spending significant time praying in tongues. Interestingly, their focus wasn't on seeking healing but on drawing near to God through prayer. Speaking in tongues aligns a person with the supernatural realm, immersing them in the healing atmosphere where divine power flows.

Eventually, I arrived in California and felt led to settle in Orange County. Things began to come together for me quickly. Within two days, I found a full-time job; within two months, I met Kelly—who would later become my wife—and connected with the pastor who would mentor me and train me in ministry within his church. Everything fell into place as if orchestrated by an unseen hand, one step after another.

Looking back now, it's remarkable to reflect on how the Lord brought such an extraordinary woman into my life. God also blessed me by connecting me with an internationally esteemed pastor who operated in powerful miracles and mentored me in the spiritual gifts. When I first met my pastor in California, I never imagined that many years later, I would have the profound honor of preaching his homegoing service. It was a deeply humbling experience to celebrate his life and legacy in such a memorable way.

It's clear to me now how I prayed out my destiny. The enemy tried to block and destroy it because he is a thief. But when you pray in tongues, you unlock and discover your destiny, praying it into existence. You make spiritual preparations, laying the foundation for the path you are destined to walk. Praying in tongues creates the world you want to live in. That world may still be in the future, but by praying now, you get everything in order and prepared, so when you step into it, everything is smooth and seamless, and everything you need is waiting for you.

Chapter Three

Total Deliverance: The Path to Victory and Complete Transformation

God desires to place a powerful anointing upon your life, providing you with the freedom and abundant joy He has made available. Any satanic grip on your life can be broken through the power of God, which is fully accessible to you. The enemy of your soul only responds to a force greater than himself. The devil is not dislodged by intellectual brilliance, nor is he intimidated by outward displays of religious piety.

The anointing of the Holy Spirit is an empowerment that drives the adversary out of every corner of your life. In spiritual battles, where only the strongest prevail, it is necessary to engage in a deep, qualitative walk with God for continual breakthroughs and strategic victories. Speaking in tongues has a dramatic effect on the anointing, releasing power to dislodge the enemy of your soul. Let me share more about the anointing so that when you pray in tongues, you will better understand what is happening from a spiritual perspective.

To clearly understand how the anointing of the Spirit of God works, we need to take a closer look at its biblical description. In the book of Isaiah, the prophet describes the impending siege of Jerusalem by King Sennacherib of Assyria.

The advancing army had already conquered everything in its path, including the heavily fortified Israeli city of Lachish. The Jews in Lachish put up a strong defensive fight, but the Assyrian army proved too powerful. They besieged and battered down its walls, put most of its inhabitants to the sword, and, in their trademark style of inflicting as much psychological pain and intimidation as possible, impaled the bodies of its leaders on stakes outside the city walls. Jerusalem lay only 30 miles away, and it seemed nothing could stop Sennacherib.

The army eventually got so close to Jerusalem that the king of Assyria could shake his fist within the eyesight of the Israeli guards on the walls of Jerusalem. The Assyrian army stopped and camped at Nob, which scholars believe is modern-day Mt. Scopus. It was at this point that the prophet Isaiah prophesied that the Assyrian army would be stopped, cut down, and humbled. He also boldly prophesied that the Assyrian burden would be removed and that its yoke would be destroyed.

Hezekiah, king of Judah, was at a very low place. He was fed up with the bullying of the Assyrians. Judah existed as a defeated vassal state between Egypt and the Assyrian empire. While there were signs of revival and indications of Jews turning back to God, they were still under the subjugation of Assyria. Their bondage meant they were forced to meet the harsh demands of tribute imposed upon them. The tribute was an extremely heavy burden—a cruel yoke that the Jews could not free themselves from.

Previously, Hezekiah had paid an enormous tribute imposed on him by Sennacherib. History records it as one of the largest tributes ever paid by a monarch in ancient times. Sennacherib demanded from Hezekiah eight hundred talents of silver and thirty talents of gold. In modern-day equivalency, based on the current price of gold and silver, this was $9 million in silver and $65 million in gold. To pay the tribute, Hezekiah sent all the silver and gold he could gather to Sennacherib. He gave the Assyrian king all the silver that was found in the house of the Lord and in the royal treasury, including the gold from the doors of the temple and from the doorposts of his palace. But that wasn't enough to satisfy the insatiable demands of Sennacherib.

In addition to the silver and gold, Hezekiah also gave Sennacherib the royal gemstones, couches, and chairs inlaid with ivory, elephant hides and tusks, exotic woods of ebony and boxwood, and even his daughters, and his male and female musicians. The Jews in the land were heavily taxed to scrape together payments for Sennacherib. But still, it wasn't enough to appease him. However, the anointing of the Spirit of God was about to change everything for Hezekiah and the people of Jerusalem, and it can suddenly change everything for you too. Let's examine the following verse through the lens of a few leading Bible translations to better grasp the ministry of the Spirit of God and the anointing that flows from Him.

> It shall come to pass in that day
> That his burden will be taken away from your shoulder,
> And his yoke from your neck,
> And the yoke will be destroyed because of the anointing oil.
>
> — Isaiah 10:27 (NKJV)

Therefore, the Lord God of hosts says this, "O My people who dwell in Zion, do not be afraid of the Assyrian who strikes you with a rod and lifts up his staff against you, as [the king of] Egypt did. For yet a very little while and My indignation [against you] will be fulfilled and My anger will be directed toward the destruction of the Assyrian." The Lord of hosts will brandish a whip against them like the slaughter of Midian at the rock of Oreb; and His staff will be over the [Red] Sea and He will lift it up the way He did in [the flight from] Egypt. So it will be in that day, that the burden of the Assyrian will be removed from your shoulders and his yoke from your neck. The yoke will be broken because of the fat.

— Isaiah 10:24-27 (AMP)

And it will come to pass in that day, its burden will remove from thy shoulder, and its yoke from thy neck; and the yoke will be destroyed from the pressure of the fat.

— Isaiah 10:27 (Keil & Delitzsch Old Testament Commentary)

And it shall come to pass in that day, that his burden shall be taken away from off thy shoulder, and his yoke from off thy neck, and the yoke shall be destroyed because of the anointing.

— Isaiah 10:27 (KJV)

> On that day his burden will fall from your shoulders, and his yoke from your neck. The yoke will be broken because your neck will be too large.
>
> — Isaiah 10:27 (CSB)

God wants you to understand that burdens are removed and yokes are destroyed through fatness. In the Hebrew language, the word "fatness" is the word *shamen* (pronounced SHA-MEN). It means fat, oil, grease, and richness. When the Holy Spirit moves upon you, supernatural strength is released. Like an ox, your neck becomes much larger. With that enlargement comes an increase in strength. The fatness contains a greasy, oily substance that lubricates the neck.

Rabbi David Kimhi of the 12th century observed that in most cases involving oxen, the yoke creates a wound in the neck's fatty flesh area due to pressure and friction. But Rabbi Kimhi understood that when the Spirit of God moves, the opposite occurs—the fatness of the ox leads to the destruction of the yoke.

Throughout the centuries, Bible translators have debated the best interpretation of verse 27. It is challenging to do so because the phrase "because of fatness/oil" is an idiom in the Hebrew language. What is an idiom? An idiom is an expression that typically presents a figurative, non-literal meaning understood only by the people of that time and place. The English language has thousands of idioms. Examples of English idioms and their meanings include:

It's raining cats and dogs. (It's raining very heavily.)

I'm going to ride shotgun. (I'm going to sit in the front passenger seat.)

The ball is in your court. (The decision is now up to you.)

Stop beating around the bush. (Stop avoiding the question.)

It's time to hit the sack. (It's time to go to bed.)

Today, we understand these English expressions when we hear them. However, if society were to advance 2,800 years—like in the case of Isaiah's writings—these meanings could become lost. We know that the King James translators consulted Jewish commentaries to help them understand difficult words and idioms. The writings of the famed Jewish philosopher and commentator Ibn Ezra from the Middle Ages would have been closely studied by the translation committee. Ibn Ezra said, "The yoke is broken when the neck has become very fat; it is a figurative expression for 'Judah will become mighty.'"[1]

It appears the King James translators chose the word *anointing* over "fatness" because they felt the Hebrew idiom represented the Messiah. We know the KJV translators were also influenced by John Calvin's translation, in which Calvin also chose to use the word *anointing*. Some Jewish commentators of the Targums (interpretations of books in the Hebrew Bible that were translated from Hebrew into Aramaic) were also studied by the KJV committee, and it was noted that some Targum commentators also preferred the word *anointing* over "fatness."

Idioms are difficult to translate when the original context of their culture has changed over thousands of years. This is why this verse can have a wide array of interpretations. The literal word is *oil* or *fat*. I believe it is a representation of the anointing, which, in

1. Commentary of Ibn Ezra on Isaiah. Translated by Michael Friedlander, 1873.

essence, is the burden-removing, yoke-destroying power of God. As you develop in the anointing of God, you will become strong in the Lord, and the power of the enemy's oppressive yoke will be completely destroyed.

As mentioned earlier, praying in tongues regularly, especially for extended periods, enhances the anointing's *fatness*—the greasy, oily substance that lubricates the neck, breaking and destroying the yoke. The anointing of the Spirit of God delivered the Jews from impending Assyrian captivity. In this instance, God sent a special angel to destroy the soldiers in the enemy camp. Similarly, God will empower you and send the help you need—often through angelic intervention—leading you to victorious testimonies.

The anointing also liberates believers from the tyranny of habitual sin and the enemy's oppression. It eradicates sickness and disease, driving them out of your body. The principles from God's anointed Word can lift you out of the pit of financial debt and set you in a place of peace where your finances are stabilized and increasing. Whether the anointing is for healing, deliverance from demons, financial breakthroughs, or any other need, it is always the same Holy Spirit from whom the anointing flows. You don't need a different Holy Spirit for various needs—you simply need to make contact with the anointing. Better yet, be anointed yourself so that you can become a vessel of blessing, healing, and deliverance through whom God can work.

This is why the British evangelist Smith Wigglesworth said, "I'd rather have the Holy Ghost on me for ten minutes than to own the world with a fence around it."[2]

If you are bound by any addictive substance, praying in tongues for extended periods dissolves the agonizing cravings associated with withdrawal. A Christian who prays in tongues for one hour daily will soon find that any form of addiction is incinerated by the Holy Spirit's fire. The only remnants of the addiction will be ashes—the harmless memory of what once held them captive. God allows us to retain memory so that we develop the wisdom to walk in His commandments.

In her book *Chasing the Dragon,* Jackie Pullinger recounts her experience as a British missionary in China. After receiving the baptism of the Holy Spirit, her ministry flourished, leading many people to Christ. She focused on ministering in the Walled City, a chaotic maze of opium dens, prostitution, and depravity.

When she led former opium addicts to salvation in Christ, she noticed the fierce withdrawal symptoms they faced. Jackie soon realized that the same power that empowered her ministry could also help these men overcome their drug addiction. She began leading newly saved gang members, prostitutes, pimps, and addicts into the baptism of the Holy Spirit, with the evidence of speaking in tongues. As the addicts prayed in tongues, their withdrawal pains subsided, allowing them to transition through withdrawal successfully.

Most of these young men lived in small shanty huts with ten to twelve people, often in dire poverty, without privacy for devotion.

---

2. *Understanding the Anointing,* by Kenneth E. Hagin, Copyright 1983, Chapter 9, *The Anointing of the Prophet,* Page 75.

Despite this, they discovered that even praying in the Spirit while going about their daily work brought the comforting presence of God. It's essential to pray in the Spirit daily, even if it's during a shower, driving, or walking.

This principle is incredibly effective for anyone seeking freedom from addiction, whether it's opium, cocaine, heroin, fentanyl, tobacco, alcohol, or especially pornography and other forms of sexual sin and perversion. The root of these struggles lies primarily in the brain, where the intense release of dopamine during moments of pleasure creates a powerful craving for more. When these cravings are abused, the brain begins to demand ever-increasing levels of stimulation. However, praying in the Spirit has the remarkable ability to neutralize these destructive cravings, recalibrating your mind to a healthy, balanced state. Truly, the wisdom of God is revealed through the priceless gift of speaking in tongues.

Victory over addiction isn't just about how long you can abstain; it's about living in a state of daily freedom, where you're not constantly battling suppressed urges. I've met former alcoholics who haven't touched a drop in years, yet they seem just one step away from a relapse. Real, lasting victory requires more than just willpower; it demands cutting off the enemy's supply lines that strengthen the fleshly nature.

Chapter Four

Beyond Breakthrough: Walking in Absolute Dominion

Freedom from addiction involves a two-part approach. Speaking in tongues is crucial for building inner strength, but it's equally important to close any doors that might be giving the enemy access to your life. It's not just about praying in the Spirit to build up your defenses; you must also stop the influx of toxic influences streaming into your mind through your eyes and ears.

Even if you spend hours praying in tongues, if you then flood your mind with corrupting images from social media or other sources, you'll undermine the work of the Holy Spirit. Freedom is a holistic process. It's not just about what you do; it's also about what you choose not to do. To walk in true freedom, you must not only build up your spiritual strength through praying in tongues but also cut off the influences that feed the fleshly nature.

A number of years ago, I earnestly sought the Lord for a deeper understanding of how to live in holiness, like the great saints I had read about in church history. The Lord directed me to the Epistle of Colossians, particularly chapter 3, verses 1-17. Despite the many good sermons I've heard on holiness and the numerous books I've read on the topic, it was through these verses that I finally found the peace and purity I had been longing for. These same truths, when understood and applied, will firmly establish your feet on the path of holiness.

It's fascinating to realize that the biblical root of the word *holiness* means *different*. Holiness signifies a separation from the defilement of a sinful world and a union with God, who alone is holy. Embracing holiness requires us to put to death five major sins within the members of our body.

> Therefore put to death your members which are on the earth: fornication, uncleanness, passion, evil desire, and covetousness, which is idolatry.
>
> — Colossians 3:5

To "put to death" means to destroy the strength of something, to deaden it. This isn't an instantaneous process but a gradual one. In the original Greek, the word for fornication is *porneia,* which is where the modern term *pornography* is derived. Fornication is a broad term encompassing all kinds of sexual sins, including adultery. Jesus used porneia to describe adultery in marriage (Matthew 5:32). It also covers all sexual acts outside of legal marriage. Fornication can be a powerful driving force, but it can be subdued.

Uncleanness, while related to sexual sins, is a broader term than fornication. It is tied to the Old Testament concepts of clean and unclean. Paul uses this term to make Christians aware that everything promoted by the devil is filthy and dirty, no matter how it's presented—whether through glossy magazines, high-definition videos, or what some perverted minds might call "art." In God's eyes, it is nothing but garbage. The Greek word for uncleanness refers to rotting or decaying matter. There are unclean or demonic spirits that influence people in these areas, but you can be free from all sexual uncleanness. You can experience such freedom that you'll see these sins for what they truly are—empty and devoid of the lasting satisfaction that comes from walking closely with God.

The third sin to address is passion, which refers to shameful desires rooted in lust. It describes an inward, relentless motion that doesn't stop until satisfied. A passion for the wrong things can enslave a person, but it too, can be subdued.

Evil desire refers to the natural inclination toward things that are inherently wrong, even when they are presented in a polished or sophisticated way, like an expensive bottle of whiskey. No liquor company, well-versed in marketing, would ever package their product in an unattractive manner—yet the allure doesn't change the underlying harm. Good desires honor God and lead us toward life; bad desires, no matter how enticing, divert us from the path of righteousness. Therefore, we must vigilantly guard our desires, discerning what leads us closer to God and what pulls us away.

Finally, covetousness—an insatiable selfishness—must also be put to death. Greed inevitably leads to dishonesty and deceit, and no matter how much one acquires, the desire for more remains unquenched. Covetousness is a longing for what we have no rightful claim to, making it a sin with a wide-reaching impact that must be severed from our lives. As believers, we each have an inheritance in Christ, but it's crucial to understand the boundaries of that inheritance. May your hand never grasp what God has not destined for you to possess.

When the children of Israel were journeying through the desert and approaching the territory of Esau's descendants, God instructed Moses, *"Do not meddle with them, for I will not give you any of their land, no, not so much as one footstep, because I have given Mount Seir to Esau as a possession"* (Deuteronomy 2:5). Let us therefore be diligent in guarding our hearts against covetousness, recognizing that true contentment comes from walking within the boundaries God has set for us.

To be holy and acceptable in the eyes of the Lord Jesus Christ, we must put to death these five significant sins. While these sins must be eradicated over time, Paul also instructs us to put off other sins immediately:

> But now you yourselves are to put off all these: anger, wrath, malice, blasphemy, filthy language out of your mouth. Do not lie to one another, since you have put off the old man with his deeds.
>
> — Colossians 3:8-9

It's important not to confuse these two categories. Under the anointing of the Holy Spirit, the Apostle Paul writes with supernatural precision. The sins we just studied must be put to death over time. However, the sins in verses 8-9 must be put off like an old coat—something you can do immediately.

You know how to take off your coat and hang it up when you're done using it. In the same way, you can stop anger, wrath, malice (ill will toward others), blasphemy (such as using God's holy name as a curse word), and filthy language. Most of these sins involve controlling your tongue.

Right now, decide to take these sins off like an old coat and never wear them again. Say this with me: "Lord Jesus, I take off the sins of anger, wrath, malice, blasphemy, and filthy language now. I commit to guarding my tongue and my heart so that these sins are finished in my life. Thank You, Jesus, for the victory. I give You praise—it is done. Amen!"

Now that you've taken this important step, you may wonder how to die to fornication, uncleanness, passion, evil desire, and covetousness. The dying process is not as immediate as taking off a coat, so how is it worked out?

The principle is timeless: anything you stop feeding will begin to die. A historical example of this truth is the siege of Masada, a dramatic episode that I have had the privilege of sharing with visitors on our tours to Israel. This landmark still serves as a spiritual illustration of how cutting off support can lead to the ultimate surrender of even the most entrenched strongholds.

Overlooking the Dead Sea, Masada is an ancient fortification where Jewish zealots made a final stand against the Romans during the First Jewish War in A.D. 73. The Romans, led by General Flavius Silva, laid siege to Masada, cutting off all supplies to the Jewish rebels. The Romans built a siege wall around the mountain to prevent escape and limited the zealots' ability to attack. After months of building a massive ramp to breach the fortress, the Romans found that the zealots had all committed suicide. The principle was clear: by cutting off the supply lines, the Romans forced the zealots into submission.

The same principle applies spiritually: if something in your life is revolting against God's will, lay siege to it. Cut off its supply lines; starve it by not allowing anything that strengthens it to enter your life. When you block the enemy's access, you take control. Growing up in church, I often pondered our key Scripture:

> Therefore put to death your members which are on the earth: fornication, uncleanness, passion, evil desire, and covetousness, which is idolatry.
>
> — Colossians 3:5

I knew God's Word instructed us to put to death our sinful desires, but I didn't know how. Then, one day, the Holy Spirit revealed to me that anything you stop feeding will eventually die. You put to death those sinful desires by cutting off every supply line that feeds them. Lay siege to those desires by guarding your heart and mind, allowing nothing into your life that strengthens the fleshly nature.

Where should you begin building your siege wall? Start by honestly evaluating how hypersexual imagery on social media is eroding your spiritual strength. If you're serious about getting free and staying free, you need to establish firm safeguards. Consider subscribing to services that remove all advertising, eliminating the intrusive commercials that play before your desired content.

But you could take it a step further: delete those apps and platforms that fuel base passions and never reinstall or revisit them. The peace that floods your heart when you close these doors is immediate and unmistakable. However, this method only works if you strictly enforce the blockade. I encourage you to go cold turkey on anything that stirs up a desire to sin.

You'll likely face withdrawal symptoms, like figuring out how to fill the hours once wasted on porn or mindlessly scrolling through endless, irrelevant videos on digital platforms. But that time can now be reclaimed for meaningful and profitable work. Remember, there's no need to wean yourself off poison. Walk away from the devil's traps—no apologies are needed.

After dealing with social media, turn your attention to movies that glorify violence, profanity, and immorality. Steer clear of the sensual pull of secular music (and even some so-called Christian music), endless hours of sports consumption, and other forms of entertainment you might be ingesting. No matter how widely accepted these things are, even within certain Laodicean churches, if it's provocative, back away and pursue righteousness.

Now, take a closer look at your friends. Do they curse and get drunk? Are they immoral? God's Word is clear: *"Do not be deceived: 'Bad company corrupts good morals'"* (1 Corinthians 15:33 HCSB).

Make a focused and sustained effort to cut off anything that challenges your great destiny and high calling. The Holy Spirit will give you divine strategies to sever the enemy's supply lines that feed areas of addiction.

The Spirit of God is fully capable of leading you into total victory. As you follow His instructions with swift and enduring obedience, your sorrows and frustrations will soon be turned into joy.

Some Christians may think that such measures are too severe, but compromised living is the reason why much of the Western church is in a state of moral decay and unable to realize the experiential life of being more than a conqueror. However, the moment you establish a siege wall, the battle immediately turns in your favor.

Personal consecration is a decision that only you can make, something that, as an individual, you encounter when you are serious about your walk with the Lord. In the Bible, we see that the successful businessman Job made a covenant with his eyes in a willful effort to lay siege to any form of impure thoughts against his mind. Job knew that his great financial prosperity was linked to God's direct blessing upon him and that any form of rebellious uprising of his fleshly members would, as he said, *"root out all my increase"* (Job 31:12). You must learn to rule wrong inward inclinations, or they will rule you.

Understanding that you put to death your members by laying siege to what formerly fed them also helps us to make a clear interpretation of what Jesus meant in His following statement from the eternal classic, The Sermon on the Mount:

> If your right eye causes you to stumble, gouge it out and throw it away. It is better for you to lose one part of your body than for your whole body to be thrown into hell. And if your right hand causes you to stumble, cut it off and throw it away. It is better for you to lose one part of your body than for your whole body to go into hell.
>
> — Matthew 5:29-30 (NIV)

The point that Jesus is trying to make is that we are to take drastic measures to get sin out of our lives. In this sermon, Jesus is using what is known as *hyperbole*. At this time, the Jews were under the occupying control of the Romans. The Romans were heavily influenced by Greek culture and language, which they loved, so this form of talk was understood by the people of His day, who had all been influenced in some way by Greek culture.

Hyperbole is a Greek form of purposefully exaggerating a statement. It comes from two words: "hyper," which means to go beyond, and "bole," which means to throw. To use hyperbole means to throw beyond with your words. We do it often in our culture, knowing that we are exaggerating and our words are not meant to be taken literally in such cases. Sometimes, people say things like, "Help me carry these bags; they weigh a ton," or "His smile was a mile wide." Jesus placed a high priority on laying siege to anything that threatens the life of holiness to which He has called you and me to live.

Pray in tongues, and as you do, blend your prayers with the strategic building and maintaining of siege walls. The anointing upon you, enhanced by speaking in tongues, empowers you to walk in freedom and to minister that same freedom to others. Cultivate this anointing in your life by praying often in tongues; it will fill you with joy and illuminate every aspect of your life. To be a Christian is to be an anointed one.

May His anointing rise exponentially upon your life. May your neck grow strong, and may the greasy oil and fatness of God's Spirit be smeared all over your shoulders and neck. No longer can you be held down by the enemy's pressure. The pressure of the oil is breaking the yoke off you now. You will walk in sustained freedom because the enemy will no longer have open doors of access into your life.

Over the years, I've received countless testimonies of those healed and delivered from sickness and captivity in the privacy of their homes, simply by praying in tongues for one hour each morning and cutting off the enemy's supply lines. You, too, can experience total freedom—don't settle for anything less.

Chapter Five

Global Impact: Faith to Influence Nations

Let's talk about impacting your world. Every believer is redeemed and positioned to make a difference. Jesus Himself said that we are the light of the world, the salt of the earth, and a city on a hill that cannot be hidden. Notice, He didn't say we're the light of Heaven—God is the light there, and there's no darkness at all. In Heaven, there's no need for salt or light in the sense we need it here on earth. Salt preserves, halting the decay, but in Heaven, there is no decay. So, our influence and impact are meant for this world, where light and salt are desperately needed.

God's desire is not just for you to be successful but for you to be impactful and bless those around you. Jesus said: *"If you believe in Me, you will do greater works"* (John 14:12). Think about the profound impact Jesus has made, with millions around the world still coming to Him as Lord and Savior. His influence continues, even now. Likewise, look at the apostles—their legacy and influence still resonate today.

Take the Apostle Thomas, for example. When I ministered in South India, I saw firsthand the lasting impact of his ministry. Thomas is buried in Chennai (formerly Madras), and there, you can even see a piece of his heel bone on display. Outside his burial site is a massive sign listing the miracles he performed in India—miracles of healing the blind, the paralyzed, and many others. Thomas' ministry continues to influence the region, with churches he planted still operating to this day, even after centuries of turmoil and war. His impact endures.

Now, think about the words of Jesus: *"Among those born of women, there has not risen one greater than John the Baptist, but he who is least in the kingdom of heaven is greater than he"* (Matthew 11:11). That's a staggering statement. John, greater than even the Old Testament giants like David, Moses, and Elijah, had the unparalleled privilege of being the only prophet who could, in person, point to Jesus and say, *"Behold! The Lamb of God who takes away the sin of the world!"* (John 1:29). No other prophet had that honor. Yet, Jesus says even the least in His Kingdom is greater than John. If that's the case, what kind of impact are you capable of making when Christ speaks such things over your life?

> But the path of the just is like the shining sun,
> That shines ever brighter unto the perfect day.
>
> — Proverbs 4:18

Your future is not going backward—your best days are ahead. The glory of God is rising on you, and it's only going to get brighter. If you're in business, your business is not shrinking; it's expanding. If you're in ministry, your reach and influence will never be smaller than they are today. You're called to grow, to increase, and to shine brighter as the glory of God rises upon you.

As a descendant of Abraham, you've been redeemed to bring blessings to the world. Scripture says, *"In your seed, all the families of the earth shall be blessed"* (Genesis 28:14). Every descendant of Abraham carries the potential for multinational influence. Whether you're reaching a handful of nations or touching people on a global scale, you have the potential to make a lasting impact. I've seen this in my own ministry as we reach over 200 nations every week through satellite television. The blessing of Abraham is alive in you, and it's intended to impact and bless the world.

I remember watching a certain Christian television network I loved years ago, about 20 years back. I thought it was so amazing, and I never imagined that one day I'd be on it. At that time, I didn't have the faith capacity to grasp the possibility. But the Lord called me into television ministry, and let me tell you, television ministry is truly a calling. You need that calling because, without it, it can take a serious toll, especially financially. However, when God calls you, He also provides. He sends the supporters and the provisions to make it possible. That's one of the key signs of a true calling—the provision will always be there.

That same network I used to watch and think, *"Wow, this is so amazing,"* I'm now on it multiple times a week, along with other television networks and stations, broadcasting all over the world. Praise God! Here I am, living in North Carolina, but by the grace of God, I've become a global citizen. Recently, I ministered in London, England, and people came up to me saying they watch me on television in the UK. And the same can happen to you in your career field. Businessmen and businesswomen, your product can reach across the globe. If you're in the business of selling toothpaste, for example, people brush their teeth in every country! Your product has the potential to impact markets worldwide because you're a child of Abraham.

Thank you, Lord Jesus! You were designed by God to be a blessing, not a burden. The Bible is God's manual for profitable living. Say it with me—*profitable, not deplorable—profitable living*. The Bible is filled with wisdom that leads to a life of impact.

> All Scripture is given by inspiration of God, and is profitable for doctrine, for reproof, for correction, for instruction in righteousness.
>
> — 2 Timothy 3:16

The Word of God is profitable. In other words, it eliminates the guesswork. You don't have to wonder if it will work—it is profitable every single time. So, when you live by the Word, you can't help but make an impact. Even if you're not consciously trying, simply living by the Word guarantees an impact because it's profitable.

> For indeed the gospel was preached to us as well as to them; but the word which they heard did not profit them, not being mixed with faith in those who heard it.
>
> — Hebrews 4:2

So the Word is designed to profit us, but it requires something from us—faith. And faith, my friends, means putting God's Word to work. Faith isn't just believing God; it's obeying God to prove that we believe Him.

Let that sink in today. Faith isn't just believing God—it's obeying God to demonstrate our trust in Him. As James said, *"I will show you my faith by my works"* (James 2:18). When we live by the Word, we have full access to the treasures and promises within it. The riches of God's Word become ours through faith-driven action.

> But if the ministry of death, written and engraved on stones, was glorious, so that the children of Israel could not look steadily at the face of Moses because of the glory of his countenance, which glory was passing away, how will the ministry of the Spirit not be more glorious? For if the ministry of condemnation had glory, the ministry of righteousness exceeds much more in glory.
>
> — 2 Corinthians 3:7-9

We are in a time where God's glory is surpassing all limits. This glory exceeds the glory of the Old Covenant, and it should inspire the way we live and the way God makes an impact through us. The glory we walk in now is far above what we've seen in the Old Testament.

So let that exceeding glory motivate you. You were made to make an impact—whether in ministry, business, or any other area of life. Step into the fullness of what God has for you, knowing that His Word is profitable and His glory excels in and through you.

God has destined for you to experience His very best, far above that which you could dare, ask, imagine, or think. The coming of the

Lord Jesus is drawing near, and we must not slumber or be spiritually asleep. We need to make the most of our calling in this end-time era. Praise God!

But if this is true—and it certainly is—why are there believers in the body of Christ who aren't tasting success or making any impact at all? I believe the primary reason is what I call the "unilluminated room of unawareness." It's a condition more detrimental than any physical disease, and we see it defined clearly: *"My people are destroyed for lack of knowledge"* (Hosea 4:6). Notice that it doesn't say they are destroyed for lack of prayer or fasting, although those are important biblical principles, which I often teach. The issue is a lack of knowledge.

Isaiah echoed a similar sentiment: *"Therefore my people have gone into captivity because they have no knowledge"* (Isaiah 5:13). Lack of knowledge leads to captivity—imprisonment, being stuck, unable to progress. It's like being in a holding pattern, unable to move forward. All of this is due to a lack of knowledge.

What does that mean? It's time for us to wake up spiritually, plug in, and start living by the Word of God. *"I call heaven and earth as witnesses today against you, that I have set before you life and death, blessing and cursing; therefore choose life, that both you and your descendants may live"* (Deuteronomy 30:19). God doesn't just tell us to choose; He directs us to choose life, so that we and our descendants may live the abundant life He has promised.

The dominion of light over darkness is instant and unquestionable. The moment light enters, darkness has no choice but to flee. This powerful principle is beautifully captured: *"The entrance of Your words gives light; it gives understanding to the simple"* (Psalm 119:130). Light is what elevates life. Don't miss that—the illumination from God's

Word makes life extraordinary, turning the ordinary into something remarkable.

> Arise, shine;
> For your light has come!
> And the glory of the Lord is risen upon you.
> For behold, the darkness shall cover the earth,
> And deep darkness the people;
> But the Lord will arise over you,
> And His glory will be seen upon you.
> The Gentiles shall come to your light,
> And kings to the brightness of your rising.
>
> — Isaiah 60:1-3

In God's Kingdom, you gain elevation—sometimes even to the point of soaring—by light. That's how you *fly* spiritually. You ascend by light.

> "Who are these who fly like a cloud,
> And like doves to their roosts?"
>
> — Isaiah 60:8

Light produces flight. Here in North Carolina, the Wright brothers, Orville and Wilbur, discovered through light—through revelatory knowledge—the basic laws of lift, which enabled their plane to rise and stay in the air. On the coast of North Carolina at Kitty Hawk, they became the first in flight. Our state license plate proudly declares, "First in Flight." But what if that revelation had broken forth in the year 1200 AD? We'd have been flying 800 years ago! The reason nobody in the Middle Ages or earlier was flying is because that light hadn't broken forth yet. You fly by light.

> "A little one shall become a thousand,
> And a small one a strong nation.
> I, the Lord, will hasten it in its time."
>
> — Isaiah 60:22

You may feel like you're not much, but God can make you as strong as a thousand. A little one becomes a thousand, and a small one a strong nation. And God will hasten it in its time.

Light has the power to make you a strong nation—glory to God! By His grace, men and women can become stronger than nations.

Now, you might wonder, "How could this be, Pastor Steven?" Well, did you know that if God brings you into a debt-free position, you're already ahead of most of the world's nations? Only five nations on the planet are debt-free out of the hundreds that exist. So, if you're debt-free, you're already ahead of most nations. Praise the Lord!

This is the power of living in the light of God's Word, and this is the impact we are called to make in the world.

Abraham had his own army—just think about that for a moment. He had an army! Isaac, too, became the envy of the surrounding nations simply by obeying God in one simple command: *"Do not go down to Egypt"* (Genesis 26:2). And because he obeyed, even though he faced opposition, including trouble from the Philistines, he prevailed. Isaac's obedience to God made him rise above the challenges and turned him into an example of God's blessing, admired by the very nations that opposed him. Praise the Lord!

You too, will experience a turnaround when you align yourself fully with the truth of God's Word. When you commit to walking in His truth, your breakthrough is inevitable. Praise God! But here's what we need to understand: it's not just about gaining access to the light of God's Word—it's about walking in that light, living it out daily.

> For you were once darkness, but now you are light in the Lord. Walk as children of light.
>
> — Ephesians 5:8

This is more than just hearing the Word—it's about making it the way you govern your decisions. Walking as children of light means living in a way that reflects God's truth in every area of your journey. It's not just a casual assumption or something we hear about on occasion. You focus on it, measuring every action and decision against the light of God's Word.

"Now it shall come to pass, if you diligently obey the voice of the Lord your God, to observe carefully all His commandments... that the Lord your God will set you high above all nations of the earth" (Deuteronomy 28:1). There's a place at the top for every believer, including you. And how do you get there? By simply doing what God tells you to do. Praise the Lord!

The Bible is our manual for life, much like a car or an airplane, which comes with a manual for its operation. If you want to live victoriously, follow the Word. Whatever God instructs in His Word is what we are to live by—hearing it and doing it. That's the key to success.

It's important to note that while dreams and visions can indeed be from God, they can also be easily misinterpreted. The enemy can use deception through visions, even appearing as an angel of light. But here's the unshakable truth we can stand on: no believer who lives by the instructions of Scripture will ever have a future without hope. When you align your life with the Word of God, you are guaranteed a great future, regardless of the circumstances.

Darkness can't build a barrier against light. When the light of God's Word approaches, darkness must flee. This is why, when you walk in the light of the Word, it's impossible to be stranded. It's really quite simple—allow the Word to dictate your steps. Don't let any person, pressure, or circumstance push you into violating the Word of God.

Maybe you want to fit in, and we all have that desire at times. But let's choose to fit into God's will above anything else. Let's align with the Word of God rather than bend to the opinions or expectations of others, especially those who may not even have our best interests at heart. Keep your focus on the truth of the Word, and don't let anyone pull you out of that commitment.

In other words, stay in God's will, even when it's not convenient. And sometimes it won't be. Jesus gives us the ultimate example: *"He went a little farther and fell on His face, and prayed, saying, 'O My Father, if it is possible, let this cup pass from Me; nevertheless, not as I will, but as You will'"* (Matthew 26:39). Jesus stayed in the center of God's will, even when it was unimaginably difficult.

It's important to remember that what you know doesn't necessarily change you. It's what you do with what you know that brings the transformation you're seeking. Knowing the Word alone won't change your life—it's acting on that knowledge. *"But be doers of the word, and not hearers only, deceiving yourselves"* (James 1:22). Those who only hear but fail to do are like someone looking in a mirror and immediately forgetting what they saw. But the one who hears and obeys the Word will be blessed in what they do.

Let's remember that no matter how hard we pray, darkness can't be dealt with unless we walk in obedience. Some Christians pray fervently yet remain in darkness because there are areas in their lives where they're unwilling to make necessary changes or face areas of compromise. They pray, but without obedience, the darkness lingers.

Jesus says, *"But why do you call Me 'Lord, Lord,' and not do the things which I say?"* (Luke 6:46). Prayer is essential, but obedience is the key that unlocks victory in your life. You can pray all you want, but without obedience, nothing will work. Just like working for an electric company doesn't guarantee you have power in your house unless you follow the necessary steps to activate it, so too must we activate God's promises through obedience.

This principle is emphasized where Samuel says, *"Has the Lord as great delight in burnt offerings and sacrifices, as in obeying the voice of the Lord? Behold, to obey is better than sacrifice"* (1 Samuel 15:22). Obedience is better than any religious ritual.

John 2:3-5 gives us a beautiful example of obedience. When the wine ran out at the wedding, Mary told the servants, *"Whatever He says to you, do it."* There was no pressure, no debate—just simple obedience. And the result was sweeter wine than anything they had ever tasted. Obedience may seem costly at times, but the end result is always priceless.

If you look at Deuteronomy 28:1-13, all of the beautiful promises and blessings listed there are facilitated by one thing: obedience. It's not our effort, skill, or strength that brings the blessing—it's our obedience. When you obey God, things flow naturally. There's no striving or frustration. It's like aligning yourself with God's ways and watching Him work.

Say this with me: *I'm blessed. I'll never be stranded or stagnant another day of my life*. Praise God!

Jesus told the blind man, *"Go, wash in the pool of Siloam"* (John 9:7). Now, why did Jesus instruct him to go to that specific pool? Why not any other? Some people, even after many years in their Christian walk, still question God's instructions instead of simply obeying. The blind man could've said, "Why should I go there? I can't even see how to get there." But instead, he obeyed—he found someone to lead him to the pool. And what happened? He came back seeing.

It's amazing, yet simple: obedience works, time and time again. This man's lifelong frustration ended the moment he obeyed. Praise God! Let's embrace this truth and walk in the kind of simple, powerful obedience that leads to transformation.

Praise God. I love the story in John 21, where Jesus gives the apostles a simple, yet seemingly crazy instruction. They had been fishing all night, caught nothing, and were frustrated, tired, and hungry. Then Jesus tells them, *"Throw your net on the right side of the boat, and you'll find some fish"* (John 21:6). Now, to the natural mind, that seems absurd—what difference could the right side of the boat possibly make? But that's the point: it wasn't about the left or right side; it was about doing what Jesus said.

Sometimes, people argue with God's instructions instead of simply obeying with joy. They want to reason everything out, wondering what difference it makes. But the power and profit of obedience lie in the fact that He said to do it. That's where the results are, and that's where the sweetness is. When you follow His instruction, you step into the blessings He has for you.

2 Corinthians 11:3 warns us not to be deceived or corrupted by the simplicity that is in Christ. The gospel isn't complicated—it's simple: throw your net on the right side, go wash at the pool, and do whatever He says to do. Mary understood this when she told the servants, *"Whatever He says to you, do it."* Simple obedience unlocks extraordinary blessings.

So here's the key point: making an impact in God's Kingdom isn't about luck, skill, or connections—it's about applied revelation. God shows you what to do, and when you engage in obedience, you make an impact on the world around you. It's really that simple. *"The people who know their God shall be strong, and carry out great exploits"* (Daniel 11:32). Strength and great exploits come through knowing God and walking in obedience to His covenant.

Now, sometimes, the covenant pathway can seem slow. You might feel like you're walking it out, living in the Word, but not seeing immediate results. But understand this: the covenant highway is 100 percent dependable. It will always lead you to where God intends for you to be—a place of great blessing and impact. Is it not better to be slow and sure rather than fast and fall off course? Take God's covenant path, and you'll never regret it.

Every provision in our redemption package has conditions to meet before it's granted and experienced in our lives. This verse is a great example:

> "And you shall remember the Lord your God, for it is He who gives you power to get wealth, that He may establish His covenant..."
>
> — Deuteronomy 8:18

Many get excited about divine empowerment to acquire wealth, but often overlook that it's covenant based.

Obedience is the validation of your faith. If you truly believe, you'll obey. And if you don't obey, it's evidence that you don't really believe. *"I am the Lord your God, who teaches you to profit, who leads you by the way you should go"* (Isaiah 48:17). You can't lead yourself into making an impact—God has to lead you.

Take the example of Isaac. In a time of famine, when everyone was heading down to Egypt for relief, God told him, *"Do not go down to Egypt."* Isaac obeyed, stayed in the land, and sowed there—reaping a hundredfold that same year! His obedience made him the envy of the Philistines. How was it working for him? Because he listened to God and walked in obedience.

The same applies to us today. Don't just follow the crowd because it seems good. Allow Jesus to lead you in every decision. Obedience is what lifts you up and sets you apart. When you walk in alignment with His instructions, the blessings will follow, and you'll make a lasting impact.

Amen! Praise God! Now, as we wrap this up, it's important to remember that every provision in Scripture comes with conditions to meet. That's profound. No Christian ever outgrows the need for divine direction—whether you're 19 or 99. We all need God's guidance, and He always leads us forward, not backward.

Don't just wait for impact to happen—implement the covenant terms of Scripture, and the impact will follow. Some people are focused on making an impact, but remember that impact is a by-product of living in covenant with God. Focus on following the covenant terms, and the impact will naturally come.

Our desire to make an impact isn't about making a name for ourselves, but about being a blessing to others. Impact is the result of a consistent, quality covenant walk with God—not just a one-time experience. As you walk with Him, the reverberations of that walk will reach far beyond what you can see today. They'll extend to nations and people you may never meet in this lifetime. But one day in Heaven, they'll say to you, "Because of your obedience, I heard the gospel. Because of your message, your product, or your gift, my life was touched."

Whatever God has placed in your hands—whether it's a product, a song, or something else—don't limit it to your local area. The Abrahamic blessing is too powerful for that! Your impact is meant to have international significance. Some preachers minister locally, and once they conclude their message and say "Amen," their message stays within the four walls because they don't record or share it on media platforms for others to benefit from. A message that could have reached thousands only touches a small group. But I see you making a major impact with far-reaching effects for the glory of God. Whether through business, ministry, or creativity, God will use you to bless people all over the world.

Now, lift your hands as I pray for you.

"Heavenly Father, I pray for every person reading with an open and hungry heart. I ask that the seed of Your Word will produce a hundredfold return in their lives—bringing fruitfulness, productivity, and an impact that transforms lives. May the joy of the Lord overflow because of the impact they're making. Raise up businesses, and may those businesses mentor and empower young entrepreneurs to succeed.

"Father, I thank You for the grace to make an impact, the grace to walk in delightful obedience. I see global giants rising—those who will carry Your light to the nations. Bless them, Father, and continue to use them mightily for Your Kingdom.

"In Jesus' mighty name, we agree and say, Amen!"

Chapter Six

Your Life, Your Impact: Creating a Legacy That Matters

> And since we have the same spirit of faith, according to what is written, "I believed and therefore I spoke," we also believe and therefore speak.
>
> — 2 Corinthians 4:13

Over the years, I've taught various principles unveiled in the Kingdom of God, but it's crucial that we turn these principles into productivity.

When the spirit of faith comes upon you, you'll notice very quickly that you begin to see results. I recall it was the year 2009, during a conference my ministry hosted. We brought in multiple speakers, including international voices, and I was the first speaker up, serving as the host. The registration was packed, and the rented facility was filled to capacity—there wasn't an empty seat in the house.

Weeks before the conference began, I met with the person responsible for the venue. He assured me that the sound system was good and that everything would be set up for our meeting. In all honesty, I probably should have inspected the system more thoroughly, but I took his word for it.

On the day of the conference, I arrived early to oversee the setup. The microphones and cables were all in place, running back to the mixer board. But as we got closer to the start time, the out-of-state sound engineer who had come to help approached me with concern. He said, "Pastor Steven, we're having serious problems with this sound system. It's very old and outdated. We're struggling with the microphones and the archaic cables. It looks like the system hasn't been used in quite some time, and we're really having a hard time getting it to work."

At this point, it was five minutes before the conference was set to begin at 11:00 AM. The place was packed, the speakers and worship leader were ready, and I was juggling various responsibilities. The sound engineer came up to me again, looking pale. "Steven, the whole sound system has died," he said. I excused myself from another conversation and asked him, "What do you mean it's died?" He replied, "It's completely dead, and it won't work at all." I calmly told him, "Go back and give it one more look."

As I was speaking with another conference attendee—someone blissfully unaware of the technical issues—we discussed the event with enthusiasm. He was excited about the meeting, unaware of the challenges that often arise behind the scenes when hosting such an event. But that's okay. I assured him we were going to have a great conference, then shifted my focus back to addressing the situation at hand.

Now, it was about a minute and 40 seconds before 11:00 AM, and I was committed to starting the meeting on time, no matter what. The sound engineer came back to me and said, "Steven, it's alive. I can't explain it—it just came back to life." I told him, "Good, go back and operate it. We're going to get this conference started." Praise the Lord!

So, what does the spirit of faith do that's different from simply saying, "I have faith"? The spirit of faith is like superglue—it holds you in a place of calmness, even if there's chaos all around. The spirit of faith is remarkable.

While it's important to understand principles—principles explain how things work—we must also recognize the difference between knowing the principles of faith and operating in the spirit of faith. When the sound system died and the engineer told me it was completely dead, just minutes before the conference was to start, I didn't panic or start gathering people to pray or quote scriptures. There was a calmness in me. I simply told him to take another look, knowing that everything would be okay. There was no need for frantic prayers or summoning intercessors. That calmness, that serenity, was the spirit of faith at work.

This spirit doesn't just stabilize your career or calling; it permeates every aspect of your life. It stabilizes your marriage, your family, and even your day-to-day activities. Whether it's as significant as pursuing your calling or as routine as grocery shopping, the spirit of faith transforms your approach—allowing you to navigate life with faith and confidence rather than with complaints about rising costs or other challenges.

> For I long to see you, that I may impart to you some spiritual gift, so that you may be established.
>
> — Romans 1:11

The spirit of faith establishes the Word of God in your life. It's something that is imparted—it's not mechanical. It's a spirit that, once imparted, roots you deeply in your purpose and keeps you steady no matter what comes your way. This is the difference between simply knowing the principles of faith and living by the spirit of faith.

There's an old saying in Pentecostal circles that goes, "It's better caught than taught." And let me tell you, that's spot on. You're not going to out-teach Paul, the greatest teacher in the body of Christ, outside of Christ Himself. But here's the thing: even with all of Paul's teaching, and even if you attend a Bible college or a School of Ministry that emphasizes the integrity of the Word of God (which is absolutely essential), if you don't catch the spirit of faith, all you'll have are the mechanics of faith. You'll know the principles—how to make a good confession, how to read your Bible, how to meditate on the Word—but the spirit of faith is something entirely different.

You have to catch it because it's imparted. Oh, praise God!

When the spirit of faith is imparted to you, the Word of God becomes firmly established in your life. Thank you, Lord Jesus.

Let me illustrate this with something that happened in my life. I love the biblical subject of wisdom. I remember a time when I was deeply engrossed in the Book of Proverbs, devouring its wisdom. I thought, "This is so good; I could spend the rest of my life in Proverbs." It was a wonderful time of study. But then, after immersing myself in the wisdom of Proverbs, I went out and did something ironically unwise that ended up hurting me.

I was at the beach with my wife and daughter. My daughter and I were about to take a kayak across a bay to reach a remote sandbank on the other side, with the Atlantic Ocean stretching out beyond it. The beach on the other side was pristine and beautiful—untouched, with stunning shells and an exotic, remote feel. But where we were starting from, the little inlet beach was rough. There was trash washed up, and it wasn't very pretty. I was so excited to get going that I didn't even think to put my shoes on. I just walked across the beach, grabbed the kayak, and cut my foot on a piece of glass I hadn't seen. I thought, "How could I spend so much time reading the book of Proverbs and then do something so unwise as not to put my shoes on?"

Here's the difference: there's a distinction between what I'd call rote wisdom or intellectual wisdom and the spirit of wisdom. Look at Moses—when he laid hands on Joshua, it says that the spirit of wisdom that was on Moses was transferred to Joshua. That incredible spirit of wisdom enabled Moses to lead three million people through the wilderness—that wasn't just intellectual wisdom. It was a spiritual impartation. The same spirit of wisdom that was on Moses now rested on Joshua, and it wasn't just about making good decisions. It was a tangible, spiritual force—something that comes upon you like a garment, with the presence of God that accompanies it.

This is very different from just reading through Proverbs and thinking you're wise. You have to have the impartation of the spirit of wisdom. Do you see the difference? The impartation gives you the spirit of it.

I've had an encounter with the spirit of wisdom, and I can honestly say my life has never been the same since. It was a total turning point, not only for my ministry but for my life—a watershed moment when I encountered the spirit of wisdom.

What I'm trying to convey is that the Holy Spirit is the oil that drives the principles. Whether it's the principles of wisdom or the principles of faith, it's the Spirit that powers them. The spirit of faith is the force behind the phenomenal faith that Abraham demonstrated. It's not just about saying the right things, though you must say the right things. It's not just about confessing God's Word, though that is good and necessary. But there's a force behind it—a driving force. And what is that force? It's the spirit of faith.

Just like there's a spirit of wisdom that can influence your thinking to align with God's thoughts, there's the spirit of faith that empowers your actions. We see in the Epistles that we have the mind of Christ, but that's an impartation that enables us to think as Jesus does.

"*Well, Pastor Steven, I believe I have faith.*" That's good, but you can't just rely on intellectual faith when you're thrown into a lion's den and staring down those big creatures. When you're on the inside of the den, with hungry, ravenous lions looking at you, you can't just say, "I have faith, praise God. Let me quote a scripture." No, no, no—you have to have the spirit of faith. It's a force, a dominating force that empowers you to do what God has called you to do.

That's why Moses could march into Egypt when God commanded him to deliver His people. Moses wasn't just armed with a word from the Lord; he was propelled by the spirit of faith. He went in and overthrew the entire system. Pharaoh and his army were no match for him. There was nothing the enemy could do because the spirit of faith was driving Moses to fulfill God's command. This force isn't merely intellectual—though you will use your mind and meditate on the Word—but it's a powerful, driving force behind everything you do. And from this day forward, you'll come to know it.

Principles alone cannot sustain a person waiting 25 years for a promise to be fulfilled. No matter how grand the promise, you can't simply hang on and wait without the spirit of faith. Imagine yourself in Abraham's shoes. God gave him the promise at the age of 75 that he would have a miracle child. But by the time he was 80, nothing had happened. By 85, still nothing. And by 90, still no sign of the promise. The only thing that changed was that Abraham had gotten older, making the miracle seem even more impossible. But despite this, the Bible says Abraham did not waver. How could he keep going year after year, decade after decade, without seeing anything happen? He could only do it through the spirit of faith.

The spirit of faith can only be imparted by those who possess it. If they don't have it, it's like empty hands being laid on empty heads. I'll say it again: you can only be imparted with the spirit of faith by those who have it. You cannot give what you don't possess.

Why do we need the spirit of faith? Because every time the Word of God comes alive in our spirit and we believe it, in most cases, it doesn't deliver results immediately. It usually delivers in phases as we walk it out.

So you need the spirit of faith to stick with it and keep pressing forward until the fullness of what the Word has promised comes to light in your life. Praise the Lord! Look, you have the same spirit of faith—the spirit to believe God for the impossible, to believe God for what others say can't be done, and most importantly, to believe God for what He has assigned, told, and called you to do.

> And He said, "The kingdom of God is as if a man should scatter seed on the ground, and should sleep by night and rise by day, and the seed should sprout and grow, he himself does not know how. For the earth yields crops by itself: first the blade, then the head, after that the full grain in the head. But when the grain ripens, immediately he puts in the sickle, because the harvest has come."
>
> — Mark 4:26-29

This passage demonstrates that God's Word delivers in a process. It takes the spirit of faith not to lose hope during the waiting process. And if Abraham had to do some waiting, you and I will have to do some too. Yes, great things will transpire this year—yes, great things are transpiring this month—but they are most often unfolding as each phase is accomplished. The faith that works is the kind of faith that Abraham had. Abraham patiently endured and obtained the promise.

So, if God has spoken, then hold on tight to what He has said, because He will do whatever He has promised. He will do it.

> And the Lord visited Sarah as He had said, and the Lord did for Sarah as He had spoken.
>
> — Genesis 21:1

God kept His word. I'm grateful Sarah stayed the course to witness the miracle. Imagine if she had given up and thought, "I think my husband might be out of his mind. I don't know why we ever left Ur of the Chaldeans. I don't know about any of this." But she didn't quit—she held on all the way through. And in the end, God did exactly what He had promised her.

The spirit of faith enables you to remain stable in the midst of conflicts and contradictions and to stay relaxed in the middle of a storm. My friend, there will be moments when everything around you presents conflicting evidence. You're standing in faith, but the doctor's report says otherwise. You're in faith, but you receive news that someone you're praying for is still struggling with addiction. You're in faith, yet contradictions and conflicts are swirling around you like vultures in the air. But even in the heart of that storm, you can still be at peace. Why? Because God has already spoken to you, and He said, "This is what I'm going to do for you." And He will do it—in His time and in His way. And when it's done in His time and His way, it's the best. It's beautiful. It's presented at the highest level. It is worth waiting for. Praise God.

To rush God is to find fault with God. So, stay relaxed. Things will swirl. Opposing circumstances will certainly present themselves, but now you understand what empowered Abraham. The kind of faith Abraham had demonstrates the effect and the operation of the spirit of faith at work in a child of God, and he did this under the Old Covenant. The stability inside of Abraham came from an inner force, and that inner force, my friend, is the operation of the spirit of faith.

You see, it can't just be about principles, because when the journey is long, you're going to get discouraged. It can't just be mechanical, following formulas and principles. There are principles we're going to work, yes, but the deeper element is the spirit of faith. The spirit of faith is the force behind genuine faith that works and produces results. You can mimic someone else's message; you can, in some ways, copycat their style. But you can't mimic or copycat their results. That's something you have to work out with God in your own faith journey.

So, how do you make contact with the spirit of faith? One of the best ways is to slowly go through the Book of Hebrews, especially the 11th chapter, and look at all the accomplishments. Some are very personal and intimate, others shook nations. Some people received specific desires despite the impossibility of those things ever happening, and they still got them—even Sarah.

I appreciate how the Weymouth translation phrases this: *"Through faith, even Sarah herself received strength to become a mother—although she was past the time of life for this—because she judged Him faithful who had given the promise"* (Hebrews 11:11). The emphasis on "even Sarah" highlights the surprising nature of her faith. Even she, who once laughed at the idea when Jesus, in a theophany, spoke to Abraham about their future child, received the promise. It's almost a joyful reminder of how she initially found the idea laughable, even denying it, only for Abraham to gently affirm, "Yes, you did laugh." Despite her initial doubt, God's promise still prevailed, underscoring His faithfulness.

Something eventually shifted in Sarah. Her husband already had the spirit of faith, but at some point, she caught it too. She must have thought, "I'm not going to be the family joke. I'm not going to be the one who is barren. That will not be how I end my life, with people snickering behind my back." No, she decided she was going to receive what God had promised.

I believe Sarah spent enough time around her husband to absorb the faith he carried, and that faith began to affect her deeply. Eventually, the spirit of faith took root within her, and she started to believe, "Yes, I'm going to receive this promise. I actually believe it's true. I saw that man come and speak with my husband. I heard what he said to him. This is real." Hallelujah! It wasn't just about her mechanically repeating, "I'm going to have a child one day." No, something ignited within her—a fiery force of faith. "Yes, I'm going to receive this too. I'm going to have my miracle as well." Even though she was far beyond the age of childbearing, even though her natural ability to conceive was gone, she still believed—and she received.

So, meditate on those in Hebrews chapter 11 who received their miracles. And I encourage you to read anointed books and materials infused with faith, not dead theology or empty religious theories that produce nothing. My friend, whatever you need in life, the spirit of faith will cause it to be delivered to you. Praise God!

Of course, you can also receive the spirit of faith through impartation. Like the Apostle Paul said, we have the same spirit—David had it, and those who accomplished great things had the spirit of faith in them.

Lift both hands right now and pause for a moment to receive an impartation.

"Heavenly Father, in the name of Jesus, I pray for those who are hungry for the spirit of faith. May the spirit of faith rise within them now, in Jesus' name. Thank you, Father, that the same spirit that empowered Abraham, strengthened David, and filled Paul is now upon those who receive it. In Jesus' name, Amen!"

Chapter Seven

Above Only and Not Beneath: A Life Without Limits

I want to share about your ability to see, through the spirit of faith, where God wants you to be. Some of the things we'll cover in this chapter might not be your current reality, and that's okay. You may not be standing there yet, but you will get there. What's crucial in this journey is how you see it—praise God. Seeing through the eyes of faith, or through the lens of faith, is key because God will get you there, but first, you need to see yourself standing in that place. Let's journey into that now.

> And the Lord said to Abram, after Lot had separated from him...
>
> — Genesis 13:14

There are times when we, too, need to separate from certain friendships or even family relationships that may be holding us back from stepping into what God has planned for us. This is part of embracing the cross—understanding that while we can always be courteous and respectful, we cannot maintain close relationships with those who are not walking the same path. They may not desire to be in places where hands are lifted in praise or where people pray in the Spirit—they're simply not going where you're going. It's okay to lovingly release them.

God can arrange circumstances, like a move or a new job, that naturally create distance. You don't need to force it; just let them go with God's blessing. Don't mourn the loss—this is a necessary step for your growth. Say it with me: "I let Lot go." Don't say it with tears in your eyes, even if you liked Lot. Remember, Lot was a righteous man but not a holy man. He wasn't spiritual, and that's why he made the unwise choices he did.

> And the Lord said to Abram, after Lot had separated from him: "Lift your eyes now and look from the place where you are—northward, southward, eastward, and westward."
>
> — Genesis 13:14

The land that God promised to Abram was what he could see, but the territory was vast. He couldn't physically walk the entire area—it was too big. Instead, he had to look in every direction and see it by faith.

Sometimes, we can't physically walk every inch of the territory God is giving us, but we can see it by faith. You may not be able to see past the ridge or the mountain, but you know there's something on the other side. You may not be able to touch it yet, but you can see yourself possessing it by faith.

> For all the land which you see I give to you and your descendants forever.
>
> — Genesis 13:15

Let's get a high vantage point and see as far as we can, because God is saying, "Yes, that's yours too—everything across that ridge, all the way to the Mediterranean." You have to see it by faith.

Sometimes, it's about physically experiencing what you desire. Maybe you've always wanted a particular car—have you gone to the dealership and touched one? Maybe you prefer older models without all the modern bells and whistles. Go see them, touch them, sit in them.

Something happens when you actually experience what you're believing for. Even if you don't have the money to buy it now, you might realize you really like it once you've experienced it.

Perhaps you dream of living in a certain subdivision. Have you ever driven there, parked, and walked around? Call a realtor, get the entry code, and walk the neighborhood. Even if you don't have the money now, you can come back later when you do.

The strength of Abraham's faith lay in his ability to see far. Although he was based locally, his vision expanded outward. That's the strength we need—to see beyond the immediate and embrace the fullness of what God has for us.

> As it is written, "I have made you a father of many nations..."
>
> — Romans 4:17

Notice that God speaks in the past tense, even though Abraham didn't have a child with Sarah at that time. God said, "I have made you..."—He had already done it, and Abraham believed it. The full verse says, *"I have made you a father of many nations" in the presence of Him whom he believed—God, who gives life to the dead and calls those things which do not exist as though they did."*

What has God said about you? What has He shown you? Get ready. God calls those things that do not exist as though they did. So, let's do something bold—something you may have never done before. Right now, I want you to call those things that do not exist as though they did. If you have debt—credit card debt, student loans, or a mortgage—speak to it. Say, "I call every debt paid off." You may wonder how you can say that when it's not yet done, but that's how faith works.

Abraham got on the same frequency as God, and because of that, he received his miracle child. But before you ever get there, you have to see it and call it as though it already exists. Say, "In the name of Jesus Christ, I call myself debt-free. Debts, listen to me—I call every debt paid off. Be removed from my life, be cast into the sea."

Now, be specific. Say, "Every credit card debt, in the name of Jesus, I call you paid. Get out of my life, be moved to the paid-off position." Don't just read the Word—work the Word! Praise God.

In other words, see beyond your immediate situation. If God says you're healed, then see yourself healed—even if you're sitting there with a physical handicap or negative diagnosis. See yourself walking three miles non-stop. If you can't see it, you can't have it. You have to see it before you stand in that place, and what you see is based on what God has said about you.

If God says you're healed, see yourself doing something physical that you love—maybe it's playing pickleball or hiking. See it through the lens of faith. See yourself re-engaging in your favorite activities.

Even though we are aware of the economic challenges in our country, don't let that limit your vision. Don't consider the economic situation as a reason you can't prosper. If that could hold you back, then anyone in a worse-off nation could say the same. Instead, consider what God says: *"Whatever you lay your hands on shall prosper."*

> The blessing of the Lord makes one rich,
> And He adds no sorrow with it.
>
> — Proverbs 10:22

Be bold and say, "God's blessing is making me rich." Even if your income seems small or limited, you can call things that are not as though they are.

Say it again: "God's blessing is making me rich." Don't let the news or economic reports sway you. We are aware of those things, but they don't determine where our faith is. We heed what God says, not the world.

What have you seen about yourself from the Word of God? That's where your image is formed, your destiny is discovered, and your legacy is established. Deuteronomy 28:1 says, *"Now it shall come to pass, if you diligently obey the voice of the Lord your God..."* The casual, mediocre Christian will find that what they put in is what they get out. But if you're diligent, you'll move to the front, and God has reserved a place for you there.

> It shall come to pass, if you diligently obey the voice of the Lord your God, to observe carefully all His commandments which I command you today, that the Lord your God will set you high above all nations of the earth.
>
> — Deuteronomy 28:1

This isn't about simply skimming through commands; it's about immersing yourself fully in them, letting them shape your inner image and identity in Christ. As you do, God promises to elevate you—not to a place of mediocrity but to a position of prominence and influence.

People will begin to take notice: "How does he or she do it? What's their secret?" They might not understand that your success is rooted in your covenant connection with God, your prayer life, and your faith. They might even be skeptical or envious, but you are appointed by God to be a sign and a wonder in your generation. You are meant to be a beacon of divine favor, as described in Matthew 5:14, a city set on a hill, shining brightly.

Consider Deuteronomy 28:3: *"Blessed shall you be in the city and blessed shall you be in the country."* Whether you're in an urban environment or rural area, God's blessing is not confined to one location or another. In fact, this could mean God might bless you with property in multiple locations.

Verse 12 assures us that *the Lord will open His good treasure, providing rain in its season and blessing all the work of your hands. You will lend to many nations but not borrow.* I declare that your days of borrowing are coming to a swift end. You are moving into a realm where you are able to pay as you go and are operating from a higher platform, free from the cycle of debt.

Furthermore, Deuteronomy 28:13 declares that *the Lord will make you the head and not the tail.* This language reveals that you should be in control of your destiny, leading rather than following. God wants you to be in a position where you are directing the course of your life, not reacting to circumstances.

See yourself in this position. Even if you can't afford business-class travel now, visualize yourself in premium economy, or even in a better class, as an exercise of faith. Know that you are aiming for a higher level, and God will make a way for you.

Verse 13 also states that *you shall be above only and not beneath.* This is a literal promise of dignity and divine increase. God wants to elevate you to a place of influence and respect, where you are not just surviving but thriving.

As you walk in obedience and faith, you will find yourself stepping into this *above only* place. It's not about arrogance but about recognizing your worth and potential as defined by God's Word. Even in practical situations, like travel or other areas of life, know that God desires to elevate you. When confronted with challenges or opportunities, remember that God's will is for you to rise above them all.

Let Psalm 115:14 encourage you: *"May the Lord give you increase more and more."* See yourself growing in every area—spiritually, financially, and emotionally. Let faith guide your vision for advancement, and trust that God will provide opportunities for you to experience His best.

"Father, I pray for everyone reading this that they will see themselves through the lens of Your Word—healed, whole, blessed, and empowered. Let them experience Your divine favor and find themselves stepping into the place You have prepared for them. May they see it, speak it, and believe it, even when others doubt it. We thank You for Your increase, provision, and favor. In Jesus' name, Amen."

Chapter Eight

Faith as a Divine Mystery: Exploring the Eternal Wonder of God's Word

In these turbulent times, the need for strong faith has never been more crucial. In this chapter, I want to share insight that I believe will usher you into the realm of supernatural, victorious living. This isn't just another message—this is an advanced class on the subject of faith, taking you deeper into the mysteries of God's Kingdom.

> Who through faith subdued kingdoms, worked righteousness, obtained promises...
>
> — Hebrews 11:33

I want to focus on the phrase "who through faith obtained promises." These promises might have come to you through a prophetic word, a divine moment that confirmed something God had already placed in your heart, or perhaps through a scripture that leaped off the page and fed your spirit. Whatever the source, today we're diving into how faith enables you to obtain these promises.

Faith can stop the mouths of lions, quench the violence of fire, and allow you to escape the edge of the sword. But today, we're zeroing in on obtaining promises. This is a season where God is pouring out His Spirit in unprecedented ways. As the British playwright Charles Dickens famously wrote, "It was the best of times, it was the worst of times."[1] But for the church, it is a time for the glory of the Lord to be seen upon us, leading to unparalleled advancements in the purpose God has for your life.

Faith is not merely a religious theory; it is a divine mystery. The Apostle Paul refers to it as *"holding the mystery of the faith with a pure conscience"* (1 Timothy 3:9). Faith operates beyond the natural realm, bringing forth supernatural results. This, my friend, is what makes faith a mystery—its ability to reach into the supernatural and manifest in the natural.

Consider the story in Mark 5:25-30, where a woman with an issue of blood for 12 years touched Jesus' garment and was instantly healed. Her faith reached into the supernatural, drawing power from another dimension—the glory realm—and brought healing into her natural body. Jesus Himself acknowledged this, saying, "Daughter, your faith has made you well" (Mark 5:34).

Faith, therefore, is a conduit that draws power from the unseen realm and manifests it in our world. That is why faith is a mystery.

Isaiah 53:1 poses a profound question: *"Who has believed our report? And to whom has the arm of the Lord been revealed?"* Faith is what causes

1. *A Tale of Two Cities* by Charles Dickens. Published 1859.

God's hand to move into your situation. The arm of the Lord—the power of God—is revealed to those who believe.

This is where we differentiate between a religious belief system and active faith. A belief system, such as the Apostle's Creed, outlines the core tenets of our faith. But while these are important, they are not what will bring about a miracle when you need one. Faith, on the other hand, is about tapping into the power of God to meet your needs here and now.

> Above all, taking the shield of faith with which you will be able to quench all the fiery darts of the wicked one.
>
> — Ephesians 6:16

Faith is a spiritual weapon of unlimited force, capable of stopping every attack of the enemy.

Faith is more than a concept; it is a divine mystery, a powerful force that operates beyond the natural to bring about God's promises in your life. As you walk in faith, you will see the arm of the Lord revealed in your situation, quenching every fiery dart of the enemy and bringing you into the fullness of God's promises. Praise God!

Let's delve into one of the most courageous demonstrations of faith in the Bible, found in Daniel 3:19-27. Nebuchadnezzar, full of fury, commanded the furnace to be heated seven times hotter than usual and ordered his strongest soldiers to bind Shadrach, Meshach, and Abednego and throw them into the fiery furnace. The heat was so intense that it killed the soldiers who carried out the king's command.

But what happened next was nothing short of miraculous. In verse 27, we read how the satraps, administrators, governors, and the king's counselors gathered together and saw these men unharmed in the furnace. Not a hair on their heads was singed, their clothes were untouched, and there wasn't even the smell of fire on them. The fire had no power over them. Nebuchadnezzar himself proclaimed, *"Blessed be the God of Shadrach, Meshach, and Abednego, who sent His angel and delivered His servants who trusted in Him"* (Daniel 3:28).

This isn't just an inspiring story; it's a revelation of how faith transforms the natural into the supernatural. Their bodies, even their clothes, became impervious to the fire. This is a powerful illustration of the protection we have by walking in covenantal faith with God. However, to fully experience this protection, we must understand our covenant rights. I don't want you to be a calamity or a statistic, and you won't be, because you're learning to internalize the Word of God.

The key here is trust. Shadrach, Meshach, and Abednego trusted in God with a faith that was rooted in their hearts, not just in their heads. Biblical faith is supreme over all other belief systems in the world, and it's available to us through the Word of God.

Let me emphasize this: biblical faith resides in the heart, not in the head. Some still struggle because their faith is in their head, not in their heart. That's why it's not working for them. Faith in the head alone—intellectual faith—will not produce results. It must be rooted in the heart, where true transformation and power occur.

This is where many intellectuals falter. They may have a brilliant understanding of Scripture, but if it's only in the head, it will not manifest in their lives. Man is a three-in-one being: spirit, soul, and body. Your spirit is the core of who you are, and it is in the spirit that your dominion is centered.

When faith is rooted in the heart, it dominates the mind and emotions, bringing stability and unwavering confidence. This is vital because your soul—comprised of your mind, will, and emotions—can be all over the place. But with the Word anchored in your heart, you become immovable, unshaken by circumstances, just like Shadrach, Meshach, and Abednego.

Many believers are spiritually anemic. They nourish their intellect and their bodies, but their spirits are starved. Then, when a crisis hits, they scramble to get into the Word, but it's too late to quickly digest and assimilate what they need. This process takes time. Just as you cannot digest a meal in one minute, you cannot build spiritual strength overnight. You must consistently feed your spirit with the Word of God.

If you want to obtain the promises God has given you, you must be proactive. Develop your faith and see those promises come to pass. Let me share a testimony to demonstrate this principle. A few years ago, we witnessed the miraculous provision to pay off our 14.5-acre Field of Dream property. But this victory didn't happen overnight. About 50 days prior, I turned my spiritual focus toward this goal, meditating on scriptures that fed my faith daily.

I spent time meditating on the book of Joshua, which is all about taking the land and conquering it. Every morning, I would wake up and declare, "God's going to do it! We're going to see the land paid off." As the days passed, my faith grew stronger, and despite the enemy's attempts to sow doubt, I remained steadfast in faith.

Then, just before the Feast of Tabernacles of that year, God spoke to my wife, Pastor Kelly, through the Book of Joshua, saying, "Within three days, you will cross over this Jordan to go in to possess the land which the Lord your God is giving you to possess" (Joshua 1:11). And within three days, every bit of the debt was paid off!

Faith must be in your heart to work. When faith is rooted in your heart, it dominates your mind and establishes your triumph. As Paul said, *"And since we have the same spirit of faith"* (2 Corinthians 4:13), you and I share this spirit of faith, a faith that is unshakable, a faith that overcomes.

So, I encourage you to let your heart rule over your head. Feed your spirit with the Word of God, and you will see the promises of God manifest in your life. Praise God forever.

Scripture declares, *"I believed, and therefore I spoke."* So, what does the spirit of faith align with? It aligns with what is written! When Paul says, *"We also believe, and therefore speak,"* he's emphasizing that faith manifests its raw, supernatural power through the tongue.

God has empowered your tongue—this small yet mighty instrument—to create the world in which you desire to live. Proverbs 18:21 reminds us, *"Death and life are in the power of the tongue, and those who love it will eat its fruit."* Everything you say either counts for you or against you. Angels are listening; we're working with spiritual dynamics that transcend natural laws.

So, determine each day to start speaking the right things! Many Christians pray fervently, but after their anointed prayer time, they often undo their prayers by speaking words of doubt and negativity. They pray for a breakthrough but then speak as if things are getting worse. They pray for health but then speak about sickness, talking about how uncontrollable it is. In doing so, they undermine their strong prayer life. But Jesus taught us: *"Have faith in God. For assuredly, I say to you, whoever says to this mountain, 'Be removed and be cast into the sea,' and does not doubt in his heart, but believes that those things he says will be done, he will have whatever he says"* (Mark 11:22-23).

Speak life, my friend, speak life! The world may be chaotic, but you can rise above it. By speaking life, you'll ascend higher in glory, favor, health, healing, and prosperity. There's a depth in God that elevates you above all circumstances. In Acts 14:19-20, Paul is stoned, presumed dead, and dragged out of the city. Yet, when the disciples gather around him, he rises up—without anyone praying for him or laying hands on him. He gets up and returns to the city, undeterred. This is the power of God at work, demonstrating that when you're walking in the depths of raw faith, there's an element that makes you invincible. You're here on assignment, and nothing can derail you until it's time for you to go home.

Receive the engrafted Word of God into your spirit, into your heart. Walk in the dominion that even triumphs over death if that's what is required. If God said so, it's your job to believe so. Go to work, start saying it—believe it, say it boldly, and you will see it manifest.

> As you do not know what is the way of the wind,
> Or how the bones grow in the womb of her who is with
> child,
> So you do not know the works of God who makes
> everything.
>
> — Ecclesiastes 11:5

God is beyond our full comprehension, but that's what makes Him God. Some people try to reduce divine mysteries, like faith and Communion, to mere symbols or concepts. But these are Kingdom mysteries with supernatural power. When appropriated correctly, they work wonders in your life.

Faith is not just a concept; it is the power of God expressed through your belief and your words. Paul exemplified this when he declared, *"Take heart, men, for I believe God that it will be just as it was told me"* (Acts 27:25). When God speaks, faith comes alive. Inject your faith into God's Word, and you will see His promises fulfilled.

> Now faith is the substance of things hoped for, the evidence of things not seen.
>
> — Hebrews 11:1

Expect to see God's promises fulfilled in this end-time era of miracles. God wants you to have a super expectancy that what He has promised will come to pass. When the timing is right, there's no struggle—just peace, joy, and the glory of God.

Fill your heart with thoughts of God's promises being fulfilled. Get up in the morning, declare your miracle, and saturate yourself in God's Word. As Proverbs 23:7 says, *"As a man thinks in his heart, so is he."* Refuse to allow fear or worry to take root in your mind. Instead, let your spirit be filled with faith, walking in the authority and dominion that comes from a heart full of faith.

You can't pour into others if you're operating from a place of fear or defeat. God wants you to walk in victory so that you can minister to others. Many believers may not fully grasp these truths, but we must walk in love, step by step, leading them from milk to the meat of the Word. This is an advanced meat class, and I'm endeavoring to feed you the rich, deep truths of God's Word.

Keep your heart full, not just with prayer, but with meditation on God's promises. Your prayer life will be enriched by what you meditate on. Believe the report of the Lord, and you will see God move in your life. When you believe, it works—it's just that simple. The key is consistency and belief in the power of your words when they are rooted in faith.

Chapter Nine

What Makes Faith Flourish?

The apostles said to the Lord, *"Increase our faith."* So the Lord said, *"If you have faith as a mustard seed, you can say to this mulberry tree, 'Be pulled up by the roots and be planted in the sea,' and it would obey you"* (Luke 17:5-6).

In ancient Jewish culture, the mulberry tree was renowned for its extraordinary root system. So formidable were its roots that rabbinical wisdom cautioned against planting one within thirty-seven feet of a water cistern. Why thirty-seven feet and not thirty-five? The exact reason remains a mystery, but the rationale was clear: the roots could extend far enough to reach the cistern, potentially breaking it apart as they sought water. Such was the strength of the mulberry tree's roots that it was considered nearly impossible to uproot.

According to Dr. Leon Morris in his 1974 commentary on Luke's Gospel, first-century writings suggest that rabbis believed the roots of the mulberry tree remained anchored in the earth for over 600 years. In the mindset of the Jewish people during Jesus' time, the mulberry tree symbolized something deeply entrenched, something seemingly impossible to remove. Yet, in Luke 17:5-6, we learn that even this formidable tree can be uprooted with mustard seed faith—a small amount of the God-kind of faith is enough to move the immovable in the natural realm.

Now, let's delve deeper, beginning with verse 7. Jesus says, *"Which of you, having a servant plowing or tending sheep...?"* At first glance, this might seem like a sudden shift in topic—a departure from the discussion of faith. Over the years, countless Bible commentators have treated this as a new subject entirely. They've dissected this passage, explaining the nature of slavery and the servant system in the first century, all while missing the fact that Jesus was still expounding on the original question: *"Increase our faith."*

In verse 7, Jesus delves deeper into the concept of increased faith by using the familiar image of a servant, a figure that was well-understood in the ancient world. During that time, the relationship between master and servant was clearly defined and rigidly maintained. Most slaveholders had only a few slaves who were responsible for a wide range of duties, from working in the fields to preparing meals in the household. These responsibilities were not optional but were expected as part of their role.

When a servant completed their work in the field, they did not come in and immediately sit down to eat. Instead, they were expected to continue their service by preparing and serving the master's meal. Only after the master had eaten and been satisfied could the servant then take care of their own needs. The servant understood this as part of their daily routine; it was the natural order of things.

Moreover, the master did not extend thanks to the servant for carrying out these tasks. There was no expression of gratitude or special recognition for doing what was required. This was simply how life operated in that society—a servant did what was commanded without expecting praise or reward. The master's authority and the servant's duty were accepted as facts of life, unquestioned and unchallenged.

Jesus uses this common understanding to illustrate a profound truth: your faith grows as you use it like a servant. Consider this: If you had a servant whose salary was already paid, wouldn't you put them to work? Why let a servant sit idle when they're ready and willing to serve? Now imagine a robot on an assembly line in a car manufacturing plant. The beauty of the robot is its reliability—it never shows up to work in a bad mood, it's never late, and it doesn't require overtime pay. Since the robot is there to work, it only makes sense to use it around the clock, maximizing its efficiency.

The same principle applies to commercial airplanes. When you board a flight, the plane has just completed another journey. Ground crews quickly clean the cabin, refuel the tanks, and prepare it for the next set of passengers. The airline keeps the plane in constant motion, serving passengers day and night until it's time to retire it. This relentless utilization is how the airline generates profit and serves people effectively.

God has given you a measure of His faith, intending for you to put it to work. Faith is your servant, designed to be used day and night. As the Scriptures say, *"The just shall live by faith."* But for faith to serve you, you must actively put it to work. Let faith plow for you; let it cultivate the life you envision.

There are believers who, if asked, "What's your current faith project?" wouldn't know how to respond. "What do you mean, Pastor Steven? I'm saved." Yes, you're saved, but what about the rest of your journey? What if the Lord tarries for another thirty years? Are you content to remain stagnant? No! Take your faith and assign it a task. Give it a project. Let your servant, faith, plow the field of your life, shaping your world to align with God's purpose.

Faith is here to serve you, not just to be a catchy slogan on a T-shirt or a bumper sticker on a car. It's here to be activated, to be worked. Use your faith to plow, to tend sheep, to mold your world into the vision God has placed in your heart. Keep faith in constant motion; let it gird itself and serve you. You've been given this powerful servant—now it's time to put it to work. As you do, you'll accomplish all that God has called you to do.

Chapter Ten

From Seed to Summit: Understanding the Three Degrees of Faith

Let me briefly introduce the three degrees of faith. Faith has three distinct levels, and the degree at which you operate determines the results you'll experience in your life. These levels are:

1. **No Faith:** This, of course, is not where you want to be.
2. **Little Faith:** A step up, but still not enough to fully experience God's promises.
3. **Great Faith:** This is where we aim to reside—where we not only live but thrive and grow stronger.

Let's break this down further. No faith produces no results. Little faith yields small results. But only great faith can produce great results. The incredible thing is that your faith can grow to the level you desire to operate in!

Let's look at a classic verse for anyone studying faith:

> We are bound to thank God always for you, brethren, as it is fitting, because your faith grows exceedingly...
>
> — 2 Thessalonians 1:3

This verse highlights the necessity of growing in faith—exceedingly, continually, and ever stronger. Each of us has a responsibility to develop our faith because *God has given every believer a measure of faith* (Romans 12:3). No Christian is without faith; the moment you were born again, faith was imputed into your spirit. Now, it's up to you to grow and cultivate it.

Sadly, some Christians seem to use their faith only for initial salvation. Yes, salvation is a free gift by grace through faith, but that's just the beginning. We're not supposed to retire our faith once we enter the Kingdom; we're meant to grow it and apply it to every need we encounter.

First, let's discuss the lowest level: No Faith. As much as I dislike mentioning it, we must address it because it's in the Bible. Jesus says to Peter, *"Simon, Simon, indeed Satan has asked for you, that he may sift you as wheat. But I have prayed for you, that your faith should not fail"* (Luke 22:31-32). Jesus knew that if Peter's faith failed, he would be finished. Faith is a living force, but like all living things, it can die if not nurtured. We must keep our faith alive to move forward and complete the tasks God has assigned to us.

Thank God that Jesus prayed for Peter, that his faith would not fail. The potential for faith to fail exists, but even if you feel your faith is low today, you're getting stronger as you meditate on what God said. Faith comes by hearing the Word of God. I like to say, "Faith comes by hearing God talk." As you hear and understand what God says, faith rises within you, leading you toward great faith.

Next, let's examine Mark 4:37-40, where a great windstorm arose, and the waves beat into the boat. The disciples, panicking, woke Jesus and said, *"Teacher, do you not care that we are perishing?"* Jesus arose, rebuked the wind, and said to the sea, *"Peace, be still!"* The wind ceased, and there was a great calm. But then He said to them, *"Why are you so fearful? How is it that you have no faith?"* Without faith, they couldn't calm the storm, just as you and I can't calm the storms in our lives without faith. No faith leaves you vulnerable to every attack of the enemy, and without the shield of faith, you're defenseless against the fiery darts of the wicked one (Ephesians 6:16).

Now, let's move to a level where many Christians find themselves: Little Faith. We see this in Matthew 14:28-31, where Peter, walking on water toward Jesus, became fearful when he saw the wind and began to sink. Jesus immediately stretched out His hand, caught him, and said, *"O you of little faith, why did you doubt?"* Little faith cannot handle challenging circumstances. It's vulnerable to doubt and fear, and it cannot sustain you through life's storms.

In contrast, Great Faith can confront any challenge. *"If you faint in the day of adversity, your strength is small"* (Proverbs 24:10). Little faith cannot withstand the big challenges that life throws at you, but great faith can.

Finally, Jesus said to the Canaanite woman, *"O woman, great is your faith! Let it be to you as you desire"* (Matthew 15:28). Her daughter was healed from that very hour. This woman's great faith caught the attention of Jesus, and because of it, she received her miracle exactly as she desired. Just as you can customize an order at a restaurant, you can also, through great faith, receive a customized miracle from God. Yes, God can respond to your needs in exactly the way you desire—when you operate in great faith.

Jesus said, *"Oh woman, great is your faith!"* Now, you won't experience results like this with little faith or no faith. This is why it's essential to elevate your faith to a level known as *great faith*. Why? Because with great faith, you can receive your miracle exactly the way you want it. Jesus, in essence, said to the woman, *"Let it happen for you, not according to what others think, but in alignment with your own faith and specific desire."* We're talking about personalized miracles now.

Great faith delivers your miracle in the way you want it. I know you want a miracle, and I know there's a way you'd prefer it to unfold or be packaged by God. I'm here to tell you today that you can have it that way, on the authority of Scripture. She did! Hallelujah!

We see that when you develop yourself into this degree of great faith, it makes the impossible possible. Some may step back and criticize, saying, "Oh, that's just wishful thinking," or "I don't know if I've ever met anyone who had it done like that." But these are people operating with no faith or very little faith, whose faith muscles are not developed. If you tell them it's possible to bench press 500 pounds, they'll say, "No, that would literally crush your chest. Nobody can do it." But yes, it can be done! I know people who can do that and more, because they have trained and developed themselves in this area.

Great faith can take you into realms where you are literally walking in the miraculous. Not only are you walking in them, but you can also command the miracle to manifest the way you want it. God will work with you and honor you in that area. Praise God! I want to say it again: great faith delivers your miracle to you in the way you want it. Now, who wouldn't want that? This alone should inspire someone to say, "I'm not messing around anymore; I'm getting into great faith!" Because it does two things: one, you can get your miracle, and two, you can get it the way you want it.

But great faith isn't just limited to this example.

> Now when Jesus had entered Capernaum, a centurion came to Him, pleading with Him, saying, "Lord, my servant is lying at home paralyzed, dreadfully tormented."
>
> — Matthew 8:5-6

When you see someone suffering, even if it's beyond your power to help, it moves you. The centurion wasn't sick, but he was emotionally distraught by seeing his servant's torment. In verse 7, Jesus said to him, *"I will come and heal him."* He didn't say, "I'll come and examine him, or tell him to stick out his tongue." No, He said, *"I will come and heal him."* This is the miracle realm!

But the centurion, recognizing Jesus' authority, replied, *"Lord, I am not worthy that You should come under my roof. But only speak a word, and my servant will be healed. For I also am a man under authority, having soldiers under me. I say to this one, 'Go,' and he goes; and to another, 'Come,' and he comes; and to my servant, 'Do this,' and he does it"* (Matthew 8:8-9).

The centurion understood that just as he had authority over his soldiers, Jesus had authority over sickness and disease. He realized that just as he could command his servants, Jesus could command sickness to leave, and it had to obey.

When Jesus heard this, He marveled and said to those following, *"Assuredly, I say to you, I have not found such great faith, not even in Israel!"* (Matthew 8:10). Jesus was looking for great faith, and He found it in the centurion.

Jesus is still looking for great faith today—in your house, in your room, in your life. He's not looking for no faith or little faith; He's looking for great faith. May He find it when He comes to visit you!

There is a degree called great faith, and it's the highest level. You can develop it, grow it, and move into it. The centurion received a great miracle because he applied great faith, and when you apply great faith, you receive great miracles too.

To achieve greatness in any area—whether it's your career, your business, or even your health—it will take great faith. There will always be voices saying, "That's not possible," but great faith doesn't argue with doubt. Great faith never begs God because begging has no faith in it. God does not respond to begging. If He did, the areas with the most beggars would see the most miracles, but that's not the case.

Faith doesn't just happen. It doesn't just jump on people. No more than large muscles just appear on a person without effort. Sure, genetics play a role, but to reach the top, you have to put in the work. Likewise, faith must be cultivated and grown. You have a responsibility to build yourself up in faith.

So, settle down in the Word. ***Faith comes by hearing, and hearing by the Word of God*** (Romans 10:17). Get back to the Bible, and also read good Christian books that open up the Word to you. Study those books; they will help you.

Finally, let's look at Luke 10:38-42. Martha welcomed Jesus into her house, but her sister Mary sat at Jesus' feet and heard His word. Martha was busy with preparations, but Mary chose the better part—sitting at the Master's feet, receiving His teaching.

My friend, you have to learn to get under the spout where the glory is coming out. When the anointing is flowing, and God is ministering His Word to you, that's where you need to be. Don't worry about the other things; they can wait. Prioritize sitting at Jesus' feet, absorbing His teachings, and allowing them to bring life and growth.

The growth and ongoing development of this ministry isn't luck or chance. It's the result of spiritual exercise. It's like stepping into the powerhouse gym of God's Word, getting in there and working out, and developing your faith by seeking scriptures that feed and nourish you. As you continue to chew on and meditate on these scriptures, your faith comes alive, and by God's grace, you move forward from glory to glory and from strength to strength.

Some of you have been stuck at a certain level of faith—let's call it "little faith"—for far too long. It's time to move on up. When I was in college, I was on the track team. As a freshman, I was in the "B group," while the "A group" was mainly made up of seniors and some juniors who were really good—fast, if not winning at meets, then certainly way up there. By my sophomore year, my times were improving, and I remember one particular day during an afternoon training run.

This wasn't just any run—it was an eight-mile loop that ended back at the campus track. There I was, running with the B-pack, about eight of us, running together, not pushing ourselves too hard, still able to converse as we ran. But 200 yards ahead was the A-pack. Suddenly, something inside me snapped, and I thought, "I'm going to catch them." So I took off, and I did—I caught the A-pack. The best distance runner on the team turned around and said, "Hey, welcome to the A-team."

"Thanks," I replied, hoping I could stay there. And by God's grace, I did. My friend, you just have to make that push. It's up to you. It's not up to God, who has great faith—it's up to you to develop your faith. So, settle down like Mary did. That's why Jesus said, *"Martha, Martha, you are worried and troubled about many things."* And friends, let me add, that's an awful place to live. Living constantly worried and troubled is not the life God intended for His people. He wants you to have peace. And you can't have peace without strong faith.

Jesus continued, *"But one thing is needed, and Mary has chosen that good part."* While Mary's name is eternally enshrined in the Word of God, your name, in essence, can be there too—that you've chosen that good part, which will not be taken away from her or from you.

In closing, you're going to need this faith. You're going to need this great faith, and we must rise into it because God is going to do miracles—great things. We want to step into it, sustain it, and build upon it. Praise God! I want to pray for you as you are reading this.

"Father, I pray for an impartation of grace for those reading, for them to step into great faith, to make the push, and to recognize that there is more within them than they realize. Their faith is there, but they must develop and exercise it. Thank you, Father God. Show them their future, reveal what you have planned for their lives, and lead them into it through the exercise and application of great faith. Thank you, Father, in Jesus' name, Amen."

Now say this: "*I walk in great faith.*" Even if you don't feel like it, the Bible says, "Let the weak say, 'I am strong.'" So say it out loud: "*I walk in great faith, and I'm going to have my miracle just the way I want it.*" Glory to God. Praise the Lord!

Chapter Eleven

Relaxed Faith: Your Key to a Stress-Free Life

I want to talk to you about relaxing in your faith. Praise the Lord. Faith, as powerful as it is, can still be susceptible to certain counterproductive mindsets, particularly anxiety and impatience. These mindsets, if left unchecked, can weaken our faith, causing us to question God's timing and even doubt His promises.

Prayer helps to suppress and extinguish any fires of anxiety. However, it's possible, especially for younger believers, to emerge from a powerful prayer session only to find that the answers don't manifest immediately. Sometimes, our prayers involve long-term or short-term projects, and while God hears every word, He doesn't necessarily bring every request to fruition overnight.

Yes, there are breakthrough days and miraculous moments. There are seasons when everything aligns beautifully, but we must also remember that faith is a journey, and projects are accomplished in phases. You may have an extraordinary prayer time but still find yourself paddling upstream, moving forward but encountering resistance. It's during these times that anxiety and impatience can creep in.

Anxiety is born out of unbelief, and it's dangerous because it can rob the believer of every single promise of God. Impatience, on the other hand, is wanting to receive the promise before its divinely appointed time. But there is a time, and you will receive it. It could be today, it could be next week, but it will happen. Impatience, however, can lead to actions that undermine God's perfect timing.

> Be still, and know that I am God.
>
> — Psalm 46:10

Have you ever considered that *knowing* is a product of stillness? When you become calm and quiet—both physically and mentally—true knowing begins. In stillness, you can begin to discern the timing of when the manifestation will come. Knowing comes from stillness. When I misplace something, I get still so I can remember where I put it. Remembrance and knowing come from a place of stillness.

Of course, the challenge is getting still, especially in a world that thrives on constant motion. But the Holy Spirit will help you maintain that serenity, that inward glow. Busy as you may be, you can cultivate a peaceful heart, making it easier to move into stillness when needed. There is a price to pay for anxiety and impatience. If you don't deal with them, they can build up and prove costly, even to the point of altering your destiny.

Let's consider King Saul. Through a fit of impatience, he committed an act that warped his destiny. 1 Samuel recounts Samuel's instructions to Saul:

> "You shall go down before me to Gilgal; and surely I will come down to you to offer burnt offerings and make sacrifices of peace offerings. Seven days you shall wait, till I come to you and show you what you should do."
>
> — 1 Samuel 10:8

This was a simple instruction. Saul only needed to wait seven days. But as the seventh day wore on, Saul grew anxious.

The Philistines were gathering in massive numbers, and his own men were scattering. Under immense pressure, Saul took matters into his own hands. He offered the burnt offering himself, an act that was not his to perform. As soon as he finished, Samuel arrived. Saul's potential dynasty was finished before it even had a chance to begin. God's attention had already shifted to a shepherd boy named David.

Samuel told Saul, *"You have done foolishly"* (1 Samuel 13:13). Anxiety and impatience are setups by the enemy. They might not hit you upfront, but if you keep yielding to them, they can set you up for something that, in God's eyes, would be considered very foolish.

Faith cannot be rushed. You can't shove it into a microwave and expect it to produce results. Slow down and walk in cadence with the Holy Spirit. Don't let others or their words push you into something where the timing isn't right. Watch out for impatient people who might try to impose their impatience on you.

> For you have need of endurance, so that after you have done the will of God, you may receive the promise.
>
> — Hebrews 10:36 (NKJV)

> For you have need of patient endurance [to bear up under difficult circumstances without compromising], so that when you have carried out the will of God, you may receive and enjoy to the full what is promised.
>
> — Hebrews 10:36 (AMP)

Strong faith is something God values immensely. It's through trials and times of endurance that patience is cultivated in our lives. Patience allows you to get to know God through personal experience—something that is truly irreplaceable. These experiences then become your stepping stones, enabling you to believe God for greater things in your life. And that's what's beautiful—you'll have your own unique testimonies because you were patient, endured, and saw God step in at just the right time.

Relax today. Relax in your faith. Your faith is working, and your prayers are heard by God. Often, the angels are busy working behind the scenes, and I assure you, God is working in a major way in your life. Stay with Him. Stay with Him and relax. Enjoy not only the manifestation but also the process.

The patient, relaxed believer embraces the Abrahamic mentality. Romans 4:21 speaks of Abraham, who was *"fully convinced that what God had promised, He was also able to perform."* That's a relaxed faith—fully convinced and in perfect sync with divine timing. When we are relaxed, we are anxiety-free.

> "The Lord will fight for you, and you shall hold your peace."
>
> — Exodus 14:14

And Isaiah adds:

> "In returning and rest you shall be saved;
> In quietness and confidence shall be your strength."
>
> — Isaiah 30:15

For your faith to work effectively, you need to relax, even as you anticipate the manifestation of what you're believing for. In this calm, expectant state, you position yourself to catch the still, small voice of God—the voice that brings solutions. Elijah, the prophet, found this voice not in the midst of his complaints but in the quiet retreat of a cave.

Also, keep in mind that when fatigue walks in, faith can walk out. When you are exhausted, it is not the time to push yourself or try to make big decisions. It's the time to rest, rejuvenate, and restore. Recognize when you need to take a break, just as Elijah needed rest and a good meal. Even Jesus took time to rest. Take your breaks, enjoy God's blessings, and relax. You're going to get there. The miracle will happen for you, not by might nor by power, but by the Holy Spirit. Sit at the table of blessing, relax, and enjoy yourself. Amen.

Chapter Twelve

Everlasting Victory: Praise Unleashed

One of the greatest expressions of authentic faith, combined with our works, is praise. In this chapter, I want to introduce you to a lifestyle of praise. Now, many of you have experienced praising the Lord, but perhaps it's been limited to a church service. Often in church, if people like the song—especially if they enjoy the beat—they'll start moving, jumping, clapping, and raising their hands. But we need to go deeper than that, because true praise, the kind that touches the heart of God, must come from the very depths of our soul.

Praise isn't just about our emotions or responding to music, though music can help us express it. The power of praise, for the most part, has been either misunderstood or ignored in the body of Christ. But when we truly grasp it—it becomes a heavenly fast track, taking us from triumph to triumph and victory to victory.

Here in North Carolina, as you approach Charlotte, the traffic can get heavy. But there's a fast-track lane you can take. It's a toll road, and while everyone else is stuck in slow-moving lanes, you zip ahead. That's what praise is—it's the heavenly fast track that moves you forward, even when others are stuck. Praise God!

This verse in Genesis is a great place to start because it shows how praise is connected to your very identity: *"And she conceived again and bore a son, and said, 'Now I will praise the Lord'"* (Genesis 29:35). This was Leah, and she named her son Judah, which means *praise*. Now, we know that Jesus is the Lion of the tribe of Judah, and because we are in Christ, we belong to the tribe of Judah too. What does that mean? We belong to the tribe of praise!

When you're out of praise, you're out of tune with your destiny, because your destiny is tied to the tribe of Judah—the tribe of praise. If you're not praising God, it's as if you've forgotten the very tribe you belong to.

Over the years, I've discovered that nothing lubricates your life like praise. A few weeks ago, we had heavy machinery on our ministry property—bulldozers and excavators—working through different development phases. Every morning, before operating the equipment, the workers would grease and lubricate all the joints. They'd go through tubes of grease to make sure everything ran smoothly. That's what praise does—it lubricates your life, helping you move smoothly through challenges. When life feels rough, praise is the lubricant that eases the friction.

But here's the key: you need to train yourself to praise God, especially when it's not easy. Just as soldiers undergo rigorous training, so must we train ourselves to make praise a lifestyle. I think you've noticed, as I have, that those who constantly murmur and complain seem to go in circles, making no progress. You might run into them years later, and while you've been moving forward in faith and praise, they've stayed stuck, justifying their complaints.

When you stop appreciating God, your life begins to lose its value and purpose. Let me put it another way: a heart that forgets to give thanks to God starts to drift into decline. It's essential to live a life full of thanksgiving and praise, because that is the key to ongoing progress in the Kingdom of God.

Now, let's dive into the Scriptures and talk about what praise really is. First and foremost, praise is appreciating God for who He is. It's not about asking for anything or making intercessions—it's simply declaring, "God, You are God. You are perfect in every way, and I'm here to praise You just for who You are." Praise is about lifting up God's name and acknowledging His greatness. When we praise Him for His holiness, His love, His power, and His faithfulness, it reflects our high esteem for God, and that causes true praise to flow from the depths of our souls.

> Enter into His gates with thanksgiving,
> And into His courts with praise.
> Be thankful to Him, and bless His name.
>
> — Psalm 100:4

You don't enter into God's presence with complaints or grievances. Unfortunately, many believers approach God with a list of complaints, expecting to enter His presence. But you can't approach God that way. You enter His presence with thanksgiving and praise. When you begin to praise Him, you open the door to His presence.

The enemy doesn't have an answer to the weapon of praise, and that's why he works so hard to silence it. When you praise God, you step into a spiritual battle, but here's the secret: God Himself takes over the battle when you praise. Every time you praise Him, there's a manifestation of God's presence. When God shows up, the enemy is powerless. Hallelujah!

David understood this better than most. He fought more battles than any other king, but you never read about David getting injured or losing a battle. He didn't even sustain wounds on the battlefield! Why? Because David knew the secret card: praise. He knew when to pull it out, especially when he was outnumbered or facing impossible odds. And you need to know this too—there are many weapons in Heaven's arsenal, but praise is the perfect one. It's the weapon that never fails, and David used it to win battle after battle.

> Let the high praises of God be in their mouth,
> And a two-edged sword in their hand.
>
> — Psalm 149:6

There is a spiritual warfare element in praise. When you praise God, you bind the spiritual forces that come against you. Verse 9 says, *"This honor have all His saints."* Praise is an honor that every believer has the privilege to wield, and when you exercise it, God makes your life honorable in return. Praise the Lord!

> Out of the mouth of babes and nursing infants
> You have ordained strength,
> Because of Your enemies,
> That You may silence the enemy and the avenger.
>
> — Psalm 8:2

Jesus Himself quoted this verse: *"Out of the mouth of babes and nursing infants You have perfected praise"* (Matthew 21:16). Jesus is telling us that praise is strength. Praise silences the enemy and brings the power of God onto the scene.

So, what is perfected praise? It's the strength that comes from honoring God. When you lift up praise to God, you're stepping into a supernatural strength, and God's power begins to manifest in your life. Praise is not just an expression; it's a weapon that breaks down strongholds and invites the very presence of God to take over.

I also love how they were saying, *"Hosanna to the Son of David."* When we think of David, one of the greatest attributes of his life was his worship of the Lord. In Scripture, we're also told that the Tabernacle of David will be restored in the last days of the church.

What is the Tabernacle of David? It's the tent of praise! It's where you praise God without reservation, from the very depths of your soul, letting your praise rise up to the One who deserves all honor. So, my friend, stop focusing on your enemies and instead turn your attention to the majesty, the power, and the goodness of God. *"Say to God, 'How awesome are Your works! Through the greatness of Your power, Your enemies shall submit themselves to You'"* (Psalm 66:3).

Yes, the enemy may be at work, but don't magnify him. We're aware of his schemes, but remember—the gates of Hell will not prevail against the Church! We're not going anywhere. We're expanding the Kingdom of God, leading people to Christ all over the world. The powers of darkness have no answer to the weapon of praise.

You cannot exalt both God and your obstacles at the same time. You can't talk about what the enemy is doing and then casually mention what God is doing, expecting a breakthrough. No, stop talking about the enemy and start lifting up the name of the Lord! When you exalt God, He steps in.

When something stronger than you is coming against you, there's a place where you need to stop striving and start praising. You've prayed, you've fasted, you've stood on the Word—but when you've done all you can do, that's when you praise.

This isn't the kind of praise that's dependent on your favorite song or the right beat. I'm talking about praise that rises from the very depths of your heart. It's not the kind of praise that only shows up when you're singing along to the radio. This is a lifestyle of praise—praising God in your home, in your quiet moments, or in church, from a place of deep reverence and gratitude.

Praise is truly one of the great mysteries of the Kingdom of God. To the intellectual mind, it may seem foolish or without value, but hidden within it is the eternal wisdom of God. Just like Communion—people might see it as just drinking juice and eating bread, but it's a powerful Kingdom mystery. Or the anointing—people might dismiss it as pouring oil, but the Holy Spirit contacts that oil. It's not just symbolic; it's a divine mystery at work.

And praise operates the same way. When you praise God, things are mysteriously handled by the angels. You might not fully understand it, but that's okay. Just do it because it works! There will always be a mystery to it, just like faith. Faith itself is a mystery, yet we are called to hold fast to it. The same is true for praise—it's a mystery of the Kingdom, and it releases power in your life.

> Let everything that has breath praise the LORD.
>
> — Psalm 150:6

God is essentially saying here, if there's breath left in you, praise Me, and I will come on the scene and begin to help you. No matter how weak or exhausted you may feel, if there's breath in your lungs, even if it's faint, you can still praise God. Whether you're dealing with a cold, the flu, or any challenge that has wiped you out, as long as you have breath, you can still declare, "Praise God!" You can still proclaim, *"The Lord is my healer. He is a miracle-working God!"* And as you praise Him, God hears it, and He moves to rescue you, pulling you up from that low place. Let everything that has breath praise the Lord!

I've even seen animals praise the Lord. Creation itself knows who its Creator is! Praise God!

Now, some people go through life frustrated because they don't understand their purpose or calling. They wonder, "What did God create me for?" Here is a clear answer: *"This people I have formed for Myself; they shall declare My praise"* (Isaiah 43:21). God says, I created you to praise Me. That's part of your purpose—praise is hardwired into your very being.

If you're struggling to discover your identity or calling, begin by praising God. As you do, layers of confusion will begin to lift, and your destiny will be unveiled. Every product's purpose is determined by the manufacturer, and God is your manufacturer. He created you to praise Him, and through that, He will reveal more of your purpose.

1 Peter reinforces this: *"But you are a chosen generation, a royal priesthood, a holy nation, His own special people, that you may proclaim the praises of Him who called you out of darkness into His marvelous light"* (1 Peter 2:9). You were chosen to praise God! If you're not praising, you're not fully walking in the identity God gave you.

No Christian is at their best when they aren't praising the Lord. Those who complain live in defeat, while those who live in praise live in victory. When you focus on complaining, it keeps you stuck, but when you embrace a lifestyle of praise, you move from victory to victory, glory to glory, and strength to strength.

Let me share a personal experience that confirms the power of praise. Back in 2006, I was conducting revival meetings in Virginia. On the last day of the meeting, after spending time in prayer and studying in my hotel room, I began to walk around the room in the afternoon, lifting my hands and praising God. As I did, an angel entered the room. The presence of God filled the space, emanating from the angel standing right behind me.

And then the angel spoke, delivering this message: "Praise is the lost key to victory." The presence of God carried by that angel was undeniable, but the message was even more profound: praise unlocks victory. To this day, I believe that praise remains a largely misunderstood or neglected weapon in the body of Christ.

Many people use all kinds of spiritual weapons—prayer, fasting, and standing on the Word—but when those keys still don't seem to open the door, praise is often the key that finally does. It's the perfect weapon, and we need to embrace it like never before.

There's a reason why praise is often overlooked, even though it holds so much power. Yes, we can dance, sing, and praise God in church services—and that's wonderful—but we need to take it further. Praise should become a lifestyle, something we carry with us wherever we go. You need to know how to contact God with your own praise, even when you're all by yourself.

Imagine being stranded on a deserted island; maybe your mega yacht broke down, and you drifted for 1,000 nautical miles before washing up on shore. It's just you and God. What are you going to do when there's no one else to praise Him with you? You have to know how to praise the Lord in isolation and tap into His solutions, His provision, and His answers.

Years ago, the late Prophet Kenneth E. Hagin talked about a man named Dad Goodwin, a Pentecostal pastor who had an extraordinary understanding of how to move in the Spirit. Brother Hagin said that Pastor Goodwin's church moved in the Spirit more fluently than any other church he had ministered in. When Dad Goodwin needed money, he didn't just pray for it. He didn't just believe for it. He'd go out behind his barn and dance the money in.

What does that mean? He had already prayed. He had already released his faith, but then he added another layer—he would prove his faith by praising God in the dance, even before he saw the money come in. That's where people often miss it. They think, "I'll praise when the answer shows up." But real faith is praising God before the breakthrough happens. When you praise God without yet holding the answer in your hand, it's a different level of faith.

As you praise, you're working your faith and wielding that weapon of praise, which unleashes God's miraculous power. God sees your praise and says, "Look at that! That person so honors Me, so loves Me, and they are praising Me even before the blessing arrives. Send My angels to deliver the breakthrough!"

There's a place where, through praise, you can step back and watch God do the miraculous. But for it to be powerful, it has to become a part of your lifestyle. Train yourself not to get pulled into murmuring and complaining, even when circumstances aren't going your way. It's okay to admit that you're dealing with a difficult situation, but instead of complaining, choose praise.

For the next three weeks, I challenge you to replace all forms of complaining with praise. Why? Because we don't praise God for a bad situation, we praise God because He's greater than the situation. We praise Him because He can resolve it. We praise Him because He can work it out—or even dissolve the issue entirely.

Let your attitude be one of constant praise, knowing that God is working on your behalf. As you begin to praise, a stream of joy and strength will flow from you more consistently, and you'll see victory after victory. Contrast that with those who complain and grumble—they stay stuck in their problems. Praise lifts you into the realm of victory.

I remember one disgruntled preacher who, when I asked him about a scripture, dismissed it, saying, "I've already got too much scripture to obey." He threw his Bible down, frustrated, as though God's Word was a burden to him. No wonder he was limited in ministry. He viewed God's Word as a burden, but Jesus said, *"My yoke is easy, and My burden is light"* (Matthew 11:30).

Outside of church, many believers don't praise God because they don't understand the freedom and power that comes with it. But from this day forward, praise will no longer be a lost key in your life. When I first began to understand the power of praise years ago, I made a commitment—no more complaining, only praise.

It wasn't always easy to praise the Lord. At the time, I was working full-time as a plumber while ministering whenever opportunities arose, and I had plenty of chances to grumble. On one particular day, we had just completed re-piping an entire house—a huge, old, historic home in Southern California. I was the one crawling underneath the house, spending hours in the dirt, connecting all the new copper water lines into place. By the time the job was finished, I was completely exhausted.

It was one of those days where I didn't even come out for lunch or take a break because getting out of the crawl space, removing all the coveralls, and then putting them back on would've taken too much time. So, I stayed under the house the entire day. Finally, as the job was finished, the sun was beginning to set, casting that beautiful orange glow across the sky. The job was done.

My brother-in-law and father-in-law, who were working with me, decided to leave to check out another job site for the next day. I stayed behind to pack up the tools. After I closed the door to the van, I had a sense in my heart—*Wait, something's missing*. The Holy Spirit reminded me that I had left my electric saw under the house, all the way in the back corner.

Now, I had already cleaned up, and the thought of going back under the house to retrieve it almost made me want to grumble. But I stopped myself and said, "No, I'm not going to complain. God, You are good, and I praise You." I made up my mind to put on my coveralls again, crawl back under the house, and retrieve the saw—all while praising the Lord. So, I got redressed, opened the access panel, and began the slow crawl back under the house.

As I was crawling on my stomach through the dirt, praising God the whole time, I finally made it to the saw. I grabbed it, thanked the Lord, and continued praising Him as I started to make my way back. By this time, the praise was flowing out of me like a river. I was thanking God for everything—His provision, His calling on my life, the job I had, and His faithfulness.

While I was crawling back, my hand hit something metallic buried under the dirt. I stopped and thought, "What was that?" I dug down a few inches, and to my surprise, I uncovered the keys to my van. Somehow, my keys had fallen out of my pocket earlier in the day without me even realizing it. Can you imagine? If I hadn't found those keys, I would have been stranded there with no way to get home! But through praise, God led me right to what I needed—even before I knew it was missing.

Praise will never leave you stranded. When you praise God, you will never be abandoned or left without a way out. God saw to it that I found those keys before I ever even knew I'd lost them, and it was all through the power of praise.

This wasn't an isolated incident, either. Years later, I was helping someone spread pine needles on a property in Moravian Falls. I had some free time and thought, "What a beautiful day! I'll just praise God while I work." After about an hour of spreading pine needles, I noticed an area that needed a bit more smoothing out. As I walked over to it, my foot hit something metallic again. I dug down through the pine needles, and there, beneath the dirt, were the keys to my motor home. Somehow, they had fallen out of my pocket while I was working.

Once again, God had allowed me to find something I didn't even know was lost—all because I was praising Him.

These experiences have taught me something powerful: when you honor God with praise, He will make your life honorable. When you praise God, you recover what's lost, and you move from victory to victory. Just like King David, who never lost a battle as long as he kept praising God, you can be sure that no force will ever defeat you when you remain in an attitude of praise.

Praise the Lord! Right now, lift your hands wherever you are, and let's come into agreement in prayer.

"Heavenly Father, I pray for the person reading this. Let a mantle of praise fall upon them right now—a garment of praise that empowers them to wield their mouths like sharp two-edged swords. Father, I thank You that this is the most perfect weapon You've given us. Your people were created to use it, and I ask that they receive this mantle of praise right now, in the name of Jesus. Amen."

Things are turning in your favor even now. Remember when Jesus was hanging on the cross, and He said, *"I thirst"?* Yes, physically, He was thirsty, but prophetically, there's still a thirst in Him today—a thirst for praise. So few actually quench that thirst. Will you be one of the ones who will? Will you choose to be a praiser and not a complainer?

I don't ever want you to lose your keys. I don't want you to lose your cell phone or your important papers. But more than any of that, I don't ever want you to lose your praise.

Take on that responsibility and honor right now. Lift your hands and declare, "I will praise the Lord!"

Now, let me leave you with an important exercise. I want you to understand the power of praising God in advance of your breakthrough. I remember a time when I wanted to go to France to minister, but the funds weren't fully there. The minister who invited me could cover some of the costs but not all of them. So, what did I do? I danced in advance of going to France. I danced before the money came in, and guess what? All of the money came in! Not only did I get to minister in France, but we stayed in amazing places—even in an old castle one night! We had the most wonderful time.

There are breakthroughs you can *dance in* by praising God. Whether it's finances, healing, or answers to prayer, you can praise it in! Dance, sing, shout—whatever it takes to give God glory until you sense in your spirit that you've satisfied that thirst of His for your praise.

That's your exercise: Go dance. Go sing. Go give Jesus a drink of praise. Watch how He moves in your life! And always remember this: if you want to see some stunning answers to prayer, give God some stunning praise.

Chapter Thirteen

The Indomitable Spirit of Faith: Receive a Fresh Impartation

I want to delve into the energizing power of a fresh infilling of the spirit of faith, as referenced by the Apostle Paul. *"And since we have the same spirit of faith, according to what is written, 'I believed and therefore I spoke,' we also believe and therefore speak"* (2 Corinthians 4:13). This verse encapsulates the very essence of why we act and speak as we do—it's because we possess the spirit of faith.

This spirit can seem foreign, even within the church, because many choose to walk by sight, making decisions based solely on what they can see. While discernment and good judgment are crucial, relying only on what is visible, especially in adverse situations, can leave you powerless and stranded. But with the spirit of faith, you can speak the right words at the right time, not only in moments of triumph but also during trials that challenge your health, finances, or family. Knowing and operating in the spirit of faith during these moments is vital.

What's remarkable about the spirit of faith is that it's unmistakable—when you have it, you know it. Some might mistake this lack of worry or concern for apathy, but it's not that we don't care. Remember, Jesus slept through a storm. He was fully aware of the situation and compassionate, yet He refused to be governed by emotions or visible circumstances. This exemplifies a relaxed faith—a sacred repose—where you're aware of the battles ahead but remain in peace, trusting in God. You can possess this faith even in the most daunting situations, like being in a lion's den.

This is why some people, even in the church, struggle to understand. They are filled with worry and fear, and when you aren't, they might think you're uninformed or indifferent. But the truth is, we are both informed and compassionate. We pray, we stand in faith, and we desire to see people touched by God's saving grace. When you have the spirit of faith, you know it—and you are equipped with the confidence and strength that comes from it.

Consider what Peter says: *"Silver and gold I do not have, but what I do have, I give you"* (Acts 3:6). Peter knew what he possessed, just as we know what we carry in our spiritual pockets. Faith is like a meal that leaves you feeling full and ready to take on whatever comes next. This fullness of faith equips us to face life's battles and is why the message of faith often comes under attack.

Jesus spoke of this: *"Nevertheless, when the Son of Man comes, will He really find faith on the earth?"* (Luke 18:8). This rhetorical question highlights the reality that faith will be under siege, especially in these end times. With the rapid rise of technology, advancements in science, and the increasing temptation to rely on worldly systems rather than God, many—particularly in the Western world—may find themselves slipping into the trap of neglecting to exercise their faith. This challenge calls for a renewed commitment to living by faith, resisting the pull toward self-reliance, and trusting in God above all else.

For instance, many may rely on prescription medication to manage their health, which isn't wrong in itself. But as believers, we should also be exercising our faith for healing. We should be using our faith to see debts paid off and needs met by God rather than settling into financial complacency. Jesus challenges us with His question: When He returns, will He find faith in us?

This challenge is echoed where it is written that *in the latter times, some will depart from the faith* (1 Timothy 4:1). This is why it's increasingly difficult to find not just faith, but great faith. Jesus prayed for Peter's faith, saying, *"I have prayed for you, that your faith should not fail"* (Luke 22:31-32). Satan desired to sift Peter like wheat, but Jesus interceded, knowing that faith is life itself. When faith fails, defeat is near.

Habakkuk reminds us that *"the just shall live by faith"* (Habakkuk 2:4). Our very lives depend on our faith remaining strong. Without it, we are left vulnerable to the defeats and failures of this world. But Jesus is praying for our faith, and as we stand firm in His word, we will not fail.

In these end times, I believe that a greater faith will be required than ever before—a bold, unshakable faith. Ephesians 6 emphasizes the importance of this faith: *"Above all, taking the shield of faith with which you will be able to quench all the fiery darts of the wicked one"* (Ephesians 6:16). This is the most important piece of spiritual armor because it protects us from the enemy's attacks, whether they come in the form of past memories, fears, or doubts. We must actively take up our shield of faith and use it to block every fiery dart, standing firm in the promises of God.

Faith is the key to achieving what seems impossible. Hebrews 11 speaks of those who *"through faith subdued kingdoms, worked righteousness, obtained promises, stopped the mouths of lions, quenched the violence of fire, escaped the edge of the sword"* (Hebrews 11:33-34). These mighty deeds were accomplished through faith.

These incredible feats weren't achieved by human skill or intellect, though those are valuable, and we certainly apply them. However, these achievements transcend natural ability—they require a faith that goes beyond our own strength, beyond our willingness to work tirelessly. There are times when even our best efforts aren't enough, like when Daniel found himself in the den of hungry lions. In such moments, it's faith in action that carries us through the test or trial. Praise the Lord!

Hebrews 11 showcases men and women who walked in the spirit of faith, enabling them to receive and accomplish great things. People often ask me, "Pastor Steven, how do you manage to be on major television networks, even in Israel, multiple times a week? How do you sustain that year after year?" I'll tell you—it's the spirit of faith. Every month, when those bills roll in, my faith is on the line. Because I go after souls and minister to God's people, He has provided month after month, year after year. It's the spirit of faith that allows us to obtain promises, subdue kingdoms, work righteousness, and, if necessary, stop the mouths of lions. Glory to God!

I would say that faith, much like money, is a universal currency. U.S. dollars work here, but not everywhere. Yet faith—faith works anywhere, in any situation. It delivers results, no matter where you are. So start spending some currency—the currency of faith—and receive God's best in your life.

Every believer needs the spirit of faith to possess the Canaan land that God has promised. This isn't achieved by our own abilities, by networking, or by rubbing shoulders with influential people. True faith doesn't rely on human connections; it triumphs on its own. Daniel's survival in the lion's den wasn't due to any earthly help—there was no escape ladder, no hidden door, just him, God, and his faith. And what happened? Faith worked.

There will be times when no human can help you, even when you're surrounded by people. God allows such moments so that you can experience His power alone. Even without connections, without a rich uncle, or a famous politician in the family, God can get you to where you're supposed to go. God can make a way for you. Hebrews 11:33 reminds us that through faith, even the mouths of lions were stopped.

Everyone in Hebrews 11 walked in the spirit of faith. This *hall of faith* stretches throughout history, and you too, can have a testimony that aligns with the spirit of faith.

Now, let's turn to the small but powerful letter of Jude. Jude 3 exhorts us to *"contend earnestly for the faith which was once for all delivered to the saints."* This means embracing an attitude that, with God, all things are possible. With God, we are victors, not victims.

The spirit of faith acts on any word of God at any time. Several years ago, about six weeks before the annual Feast of Tabernacles, I felt a strong urging from God to receive a special offering to pay off the remaining balance on our ministry land. I thought, "Lord, it would take a miracle." And He said, "You do your part and believe Me." So, we received the offering, without pressure or gimmicks, just simple faith. And without any sleepless nights, without anxiety, all the money came in, and the land was paid off in full. Can you say, "Glory to God"! Hallelujah!

The spirit of faith delivers without gimmicks or tricks. You need the spirit of faith to operate in the realm of being more than a conqueror. At the close of this chapter, I'm going to pray for you to receive a fresh impartation of the spirit of faith.

The spirit of faith can fall upon multitudes simultaneously. Numbers 11:16-17 illustrates how the spirit that was on Moses was imparted to 70 elders. Similarly, in Philippians 1:7, Paul says that the grace upon his life was extended to the entire church in Philippi. The spirit of faith can be transferred and imparted to many. Romans 1:11 tells us that the spirit of faith establishes you in the things of God, and Paul could impart that to the church in Rome.

One thing that has helped me sustain the spirit of faith is reading biographies of men and women who operated in that same spirit. Stories of those who overcame great odds because of their faith in God have inspired me deeply.

For example, Peter J. Daniels, an illiterate bricklayer, gave his life to Jesus after hearing Billy Graham preach in Australia. He then read over 5,000 biographies of great people who overcame impossible odds. That spirit of faith began to touch him, and he went on to become a billionaire in real estate. What a powerful testimony!

In 2 Timothy 4:13, we see that Paul was a reader too. He requested his books and parchments, which likely included writings that illuminated the Scriptures. Paul, with his vast knowledge of the Word of God, still sought out materials that carried the spirit of faith. If Paul found value in such resources, so should we.

> And in Your majesty ride prosperously because of truth,
> humility, and righteousness;
> And Your right hand shall teach You awesome things.
>
> — Psalm 45:4

The spirit of faith carries you from one level of victory to another, driven by the revelation of God's Word in your life. You must keep looking forward, continually stimulating and exercising the spirit of faith. Praise the Lord.

Now, lift your right hand and receive this prayer. "Heavenly Father, I pray for those reading right now. I ask that you fill them with a fresh infilling of the spirit of faith. Some may be feeling fatigued, distracted, or even discouraged by the many challenges they've faced—challenges they didn't anticipate. But, Father, I thank you for the great miracles you're going to perform in their lives.

"Father, we recognize that while some things may be in the future, our faith and expectancy are engaged for them now. We thank You, for You're moving swiftly, and doing things in months that would typically take years. If You created the entire universe and everything in it within six days, there's nothing that Your people need or desire that You cannot accomplish swiftly. Father, we thank You. We receive the spirit of faith in Jesus' name. Amen. Glory to God."

Let me ask you this—do you believe God can do it? I know you do. I know you believe in God's power. The spirit of faith not only declares that God will do it, but also ignites the faith necessary to receive it. Watch as God accelerates things greatly in your life. He doesn't need 20 years—He can do it very, very quickly. I believe He will, and I look forward to hearing your testimonies.

Chapter Fourteen

Seven Unique Manifestations of the Spirit of Faith

I want to share with you the power of achieving the impossible—those feats many deem unachievable or out of reach. History shows us that what was once considered impossible has often become reality. I truly believe you are destined for even greater breakthroughs, surpassing boundaries and redefining what's possible.

> And since we have the same spirit of faith, according to what is written, "I believed and therefore I spoke," we also believe and therefore speak.
>
> — 2 Corinthians 4:13

The spirit of faith empowers you to do what others say cannot be done. It enables you to experience ongoing breakthroughs—new breakthroughs every week. The spirit of faith allows you to see the invisible.

> But the righteousness of faith speaks in this way, "Do not say in your heart, 'Who will ascend into heaven?'" (that is, to bring Christ down from above) or, "'Who will descend into the abyss?'" (that is, to bring Christ up from the dead). But what does it say? "The word is near you, in your mouth and in your heart" (that is, the word of faith which we preach).
>
> — Romans 10:6-8

We operate by the spirit of faith, and when we do, we connect with God's power. As a result, we accomplish what others deem impossible. While they are in unbelief, we are over here, getting it done! Praise God!

> By faith they passed through the Red Sea as by dry land, whereas the Egyptians, attempting to do so, were drowned.
>
> — Hebrews 11:29

On that day, every single Israelite was filled with the spirit of faith, and it empowered them to pass through the Red Sea. Imagine the awe of looking up at those massive walls of water on each side. Every single Israelite made it through, but every single Egyptian, lacking that spirit of faith, was drowned. The spirit of faith allows you to navigate through the challenges of this world and accomplish the impossible.

The spirit of faith is also transgenerational, moving from one generation to the next. Throughout history, there have been great men and women who walked with the spirit of faith, and being around them allowed that faith to naturally rub off on others. That's what's happening now—the spirit of faith that has been passed down is reaching you, helping to build and strengthen your own faith.

Not every Christian carries the spirit of faith. Many believers have faith to be born again, but they never use their faith for anything else. They go through life with a "woe is me" mentality, not understanding that they are overcomers, more than conquerors. But the spirit of faith is available to all who are willing to receive it and walk in it.

> One generation shall praise Your works to another,
> And shall declare Your mighty acts.
>
> — Psalm 145:4

Growing up, I never heard testimonies of God giving breakthroughs. I never heard someone say in church, "*God blessed me with a great job because we prayed and believed.*" Why? Because the denomination I was raised in didn't believe in miracles, speaking in tongues, or the power of the Spirit. We were steeped in religious tradition, a man-made tradition that can rob people of their inheritance in God's blessings.

But I'm here to tell you today that the spirit of faith is real, and it is powerful. It's time to embrace it, walk in it, and do the impossible.

There was a time in my life when I had never encountered the spirit of faith. Without it, we were left in survival mode—just getting by, with the hope that if anything happened, at least we were saved and would eventually make it to Heaven. But when it came to living in victory—over sin, temptation, and the relentless challenges thrown at us by the world—we were woefully unequipped. We loved God, but we didn't have the spiritual armor needed to stand against the onslaught of Hell that the Church faces daily. As a result, there were many casualties, many sorrows, and countless tears shed in those small country churches where I grew up. Tragedy was common, but powerful testimonies were nonexistent. Why? Because we had no clue about the spirit of faith.

I never saw it in any preacher I encountered. Sure, I witnessed evangelistic anointings and heard strong sermons encouraging us to live for God. But I never saw the spirit of faith that proclaims, "We can overcome, we can succeed, and we're going to get this thing done!" That kind of talk was foreign to me.

But here's the truth: there are millions of Christians around the world sitting in dead, religious churches, just like the ones I grew up in, and they don't know about the spirit of faith. They are living in defeat, simply because they've never encountered it. When you embrace the spirit of faith, you'll find yourself with a testimony that says, "Look what God has done!" You'll no longer be defeated. Instead, you'll be living in victory.

I once heard a woman trying to give a testimony in a church service, but she stopped in the middle of it and said, "I don't even know what I'm doing. I'm torn up from the floor up; I'm so messed up." She started getting hysterical, and the pastor had to sit her down and calm her. Why? Because she had a defeated mentality. This is a perfect example of what happens when people lack the spirit of faith.

"One generation shall praise Your works to another, and shall declare Your mighty acts" (Psalm 145:4). When you walk in the spirit of faith, you

will have those around you—those coming up beneath you—who will hear you constantly praising God. You'll be telling them all the time, "God is a good God. He did it for me, and He'll do it for you. He did it for Abraham. He did it for David. And He'll do it for you because He's the same God!" The spirit of faith that was on Moses, that was on Paul, is on you. Praise the Lord! And others will notice something different about you because not every believer walks in that spirit.

Now, let's take a look at the heroes of faith listed in Hebrews chapter 11. Each of them had their own faith testimony that spoke to the new generation that followed. Let's focus on Abraham for a moment.

> By faith Abraham obeyed when he was called to go out to the place which he would receive as an inheritance. And he went out, not knowing where he was going.
>
> — Hebrews 11:8

Not too many people would be willing to do that. That's why Abraham is known as the father of faith—because he actually did it. He didn't demand a map or ask for all the details before he took the first step. He simply obeyed, trusting God every step of the way. He walked by faith, not by sight.

Abraham's journey from the Ur of the Chaldeans to the land we now know as Israel was a journey of faith. God didn't show him everything upfront; instead, He guided Abraham step by step, just as He guides us today. The spirit of faith leads us in the direction of what God wants us to accomplish. Abraham left his home without knowing his final destination, but he was essentially saying, "God, as You show me, I'll go." And he kept on walking, trusting God with every step. That's not regular faith—that's the spirit of faith at work.

And this is how the spirit of faith operates in our lives today. God may not show you everything at once, but as you take those steps of faith, He will guide you. This is also how the spiritual gifts operate. When you receive a word of knowledge or a prophetic word, God may not give you everything upfront. But as you obey and move forward, more begins to come. It all works on a faith basis.

So, let's walk in the spirit of faith. Let's embrace it, live by it, and watch as God leads us to accomplish the impossible.

> By faith Noah, being divinely warned of things not yet seen, moved with godly fear, prepared an ark...
>
> — Hebrews 11:7

Think about that—Noah was moved with godly fear. There are times when God lights a fire in you, and you feel like you've got to work all night, and you don't even mind. Why? Because something is burning on the inside of you. You are being moved or driven by the Spirit of God, and it's good! It's the same fire that Jeremiah spoke of, saying it was *"like a fire shut up in my bones"* (Jeremiah 20:9). That's the spirit of faith in action.

Let me share seven unique manifestations of the spirit of faith—powerful forces that will ignite within you the courage and determination to achieve what others believe to be impossible. These manifestations will inspire, strengthen, and guide you to rise above limitations and bring extraordinary visions to life.

1. The spirit of faith is a spirit of dominion.

This is why the spirit of faith is so essential—it empowers us to confront and overcome opposition. *"Who through faith subdued kingdoms..."* (Hebrews 11:33). To subdue a kingdom is to take dominion over it. The spirit of faith places you in a position of authority, enabling you to subdue kingdoms, work righteousness, obtain promises, and even stop the mouths of lions. This is dominion in action: taking control of situations that others would deem impossible.

The spirit of faith equips you not merely to endure life's challenges but to conquer and shape them. This authority finds its roots in God's original mandate to Adam and Eve to *have dominion* over the earth. Like them, we are called to exercise dominion, not to succumb to the pressures of life but to rise above them and bring them into alignment with God's will.

Then God said, *"Let Us make man in Our image, according to Our likeness; let them have dominion over the fish of the sea, over the birds of the air, and over the cattle, over all the earth and over every creeping thing that creeps on the earth"* (Genesis 1:26).

God has given us the authority to take dominion over the "creepy crawlies" of life—whether they are literal pests or figurative challenges that try to unsettle us. We are called to subdue anything that stands in our way, whether minor inconveniences or major obstacles. Jesus paid a high price for this dominion, and it's through the spirit of faith that we activate it. Use your faith to subdue every challenge, overcome every obstacle, and walk in dominion over your circumstances.

2. The spirit of faith empowers us to "believe all things" that are written in the Bible, all that God has said.

> But this I confess to you, that according to the Way which they call a sect, so I worship the God of my fathers, believing all things which are written in the Law and in the Prophets.
>
> — Acts 24:14

Today, we have atheistic theologians and seminarian professors who don't believe in the virgin birth of Christ through Mary and intellectuals within the church who claim that stories like Jonah being swallowed by a great fish are just fiction. But Paul said he believed *all things* written in the Law and the Prophets. My friend, I believe the Bible—all of it. I believe the Egyptians drowned in the Red Sea. I believe the Israelites passed through on dry ground. I believe Jonah was swallowed by a large fish and spent three days and three nights in its belly before being spewed out to preach in Nineveh.

Archaeologists skilled with a spade but lacking in faith used to claim that Nineveh didn't exist, dismissing it as a fictitious city. But now, there it lies in Iraq, in Mosul, for the whole world to see, even with inscriptions in the king's own chamber verifying its identity. I believe the Bible. Say it with me: *"Let God be true and every man a liar who doesn't agree with God's Word."* Amen! How do you believe like that? By the spirit of faith!

It's shocking when you go to Israel and find that many leading archaeologists, those working with the government-recognized antiquities agency, are predominantly atheists. They're Jews with the same Old Testament scriptures we have, yet they don't believe it, even when archaeology proves its truth. They make excuses, saying, *"Well, we still really don't know... it could be this, or maybe that."* Why all the doubt? Because they don't have the spirit of faith, and without it, they can't believe. But we believe because we have the same spirit—the same spirit that was on Moses, on Joshua, on David, and on Peter and Paul. That spirit is on you and me! Praise God!

3. The spirit of faith creates a powerful partnership with God.

The spirit of faith isn't just something you keep inside yourself; it creates a powerful partnership between you and God. Imagine it like a business partnership. You bring your trust, obedience, and actions, and God provides His unlimited power and resources. When you step out in faith, God's power backs you up, making it possible to achieve things you could never do on your own.

For example, in Hebrews 11:29, the people of Israel passed through the Red Sea by faith, while the Egyptians, who lacked faith, were drowned. The difference was their partnership with God through faith. This illustrates how the spirit of faith connects you to God's strength and enables you to overcome otherwise impossible challenges.

Romans 11:17-20 further explains that as believers, we are grafted into God's promises. We don't stand by our own strength, but by our faith, which links us to God's unfailing power. Anything that cannot defeat God cannot defeat us because we are united with Him through the spirit of faith.

4. The spirit of faith draws on God's power whenever needed.

The spirit of faith gives you access to God's power whenever you need it. Whenever you face a challenge, the spirit of faith allows you to draw on God's strength and solutions. God's Word is described as *"living and powerful"* (Hebrews 4:12), meaning it's not just words on a page but a spiritual source of divine power that you can activate whenever you need it.

By standing firmly on God's Word in faith, you activate His power to work in your life. The enemy trembles at the Word of God because it is alive, powerful, and sharper than any two-edged sword, capable of cutting through every barrier and dismantling every stronghold. Just as ancient warriors mastered their swords to triumph in battle, you too, can skillfully wield the Word of God as your weapon of victory. With it, you can confront challenges and step into the fullness of God's promises for your life. The spirit of faith becomes the channel through which God's power flows into every situation you face.

5. The spirit of faith brings divine help and intervention.

> And when he heard that it was Jesus of Nazareth, he began to cry out and say, "Jesus, Son of David, have mercy on me!"
>
> — Mark 10:47

This account refers to blind Bartimaeus, who, upon hearing that Jesus was nearby, cried out for mercy. Bartimaeus' cry wasn't just a plea; it was a powerful act of faith. His belief in Jesus' ability to heal, coupled with his recognition of Jesus' messianic identity, was rooted in what he had heard about Him—demonstrating that faith indeed comes by hearing the Word of God.

Jesus responded immediately to Bartimaeus' cry. Despite the fickleness of the crowd—crowds are often unstable and can change their attitudes quickly—Jesus stood still. This illustrates how God is attracted by the spirit of faith. Jesus then commanded that Bartimaeus be called, again demonstrating that divine intervention frequently occurs when the spirit of faith is expressed.

Jesus asked Bartimaeus, *"What do you want me to do for you?"* Bartimaeus replied, *"Rabboni, that I may receive my sight"* (Mark 10:51). Jesus' response was immediate; Bartimaeus received his sight right then and there. This moment shows how the spirit of faith brings divine intervention into personal situations, resulting in miraculous outcomes.

> Immediately many gathered together, so that there was no longer room to receive them, not even near the door. And He preached the word to them.
>
> — Mark 2:2

When Jesus attracted a crowd, He didn't engage in entertainment or distraction. Instead, He focused on preaching the Word. The story continues with four men bringing a paralytic on a mat. Because the house was so crowded, they couldn't get in through the door, so they made a dramatic decision to lower the man through an opening they made in the roof.

This action highlights a timeless principle that the Lord revealed to me: "When your faith is ready, your four men will show up." This means that when your faith is prepared and active, the necessary help will come. The four men who helped lower the paralytic were essential for the miracle; their presence and willingness were divinely orchestrated. It wasn't a coincidence but a result of the paralytic's faith.

Jesus, despite the disruption, continued to preach. This demonstrates that not every disturbance is necessarily from the devil. Sometimes, divine disturbances are part of God's plan. Jesus managed to preach through the commotion of the roof being taken off, indicating His ability to flow with the Holy Spirit amidst unexpected events.

As you move in the spirit of faith, expect divine intervention to manifest in your situation. Whether you need someone with a specific skill, a favor, or a blessing, God can provide it. Walking in the spirit of faith always makes divine intervention within reach, transforming challenges into opportunities for extraordinary victories.

6. A person with the spirit of faith overcomes the world.

Faith is the key to overcoming any challenge the world throws at you. Faith is a powerful force that empowers you for dominion, and a key aspect of this power is that whatever is born of God overcomes the world. As a believer, you are born of God, and this fundamental truth means you have the inherent ability to triumph over worldly challenges.

> For whatever is born of God overcomes the world. And this is the victory that has overcome the world—our faith.
>
> — 1 John 5:4

This verse underscores that your faith is the victory that allows you to overcome the world. The *world* here includes the worldly systems and all the sins, traps, and snares that the enemy uses, such as the lust of the eyes, the lust of the flesh, and the arrogant pride of life. These are the tools the adversary uses to entangle and derail believers from their purpose. Operating in the spirit of faith grants you the power to overcome these challenges.

> "'Rise, take your journey, and cross over the River Arnon. Look, I have given into your hand Sihon the Amorite, king of Heshbon, and his land. Begin to possess it, and engage him in battle.'"
>
> — Deuteronomy 2:24

This passage demonstrates that God had already delivered the land, giants, and fortified strongholds into the hands of His people. It's a powerful reminder that when God makes a promise, He equips you with the authority and ability to claim it, no matter the challenges or opposition in your way.

Walking in the spirit of faith is like drawing a sword from its sheath—it emboldens you to rise up, take decisive action, and confront whatever stands between you and God's promises. The spirit of faith empowers you to engage in the battle with confidence, knowing that victory is assured because God has gone before you. Your part is to step forward, trust His Word, and seize what He has already prepared for you.

It's important to understand that every believer's promised land will have giants. But with the spirit of faith, you have a powerful weapon to overcome these giants. As you wield your sword of faith, you confront and subdue these challenges, knowing that faith is the antidote to fear.

Jesus asked: *"Why are you so fearful? How is it that you have no faith?"* (Mark 4:40). Fear is essentially a byproduct of a lack of faith. When you are strong in faith, fear loses its grip on you. Your faith enables you to fight the good fight and overcome the world's challenges. As you stand firm in the spirit of faith, you will find that the spirit of fear diminishes, and you become empowered to achieve victory.

7. The spirit of faith activates God's integrity to fulfill His Word.

The believer who has the spirit of faith will move God to fulfill His promises. When you stand in faith, you are activating God's integrity to bring His Word to pass in your life. *"If we are faithless, He remains faithful; He cannot deny Himself"* (2 Timothy 2:13). Even when we waver, God's faithfulness remains the same.

God's Word is true, and His commitment to it is unwavering. Even if our faith wavers, God's integrity remains intact. He cannot and will not deny Himself. When you stand in agreement with His Word, you tap into His divine faithfulness.

The spirit of faith becomes active and strong when you dive deep into any biblical topic. When a particular scripture sparks your faith, it brings the Word of God to life within you. At that moment, God's integrity is committed to bringing that Word to pass in your life. His Word is alive and active, and as you consume it, just like food nourishes the body, it will quicken your spirit. When you stand firm on His Word, God sees your faith and commits to fulfilling His promises.

However, any genuine word from God will challenge you in this area, as Scripture reveals:

> Until the time that his word came to pass,
> The word of the Lord tested him.
>
> — Psalm 105:19

It's important to note that it wasn't the devil who tested Joseph—it was God. The Hebrew word for *tested* (*tsaraph*) conveys the idea of refining or purifying, much like the process of removing impurities from metals. This testing wasn't for God's benefit—He is perfect in every way—but for Joseph's growth and preparation.

In Joseph's life, the trials he endured—betrayal by his brothers, slavery in a foreign land, and imprisonment due to false accusations—were the very tools God used to refine his character and prepare him for the monumental leadership role ahead. While God's promises are always sure, the path to their fulfillment often involves a season of testing and refinement. It is essential that the spirit of faith be kept burning within your heart during these times.

The spirit of faith manifests in seven transformative ways. It empowers dominion, enabling believers to overcome challenges and align circumstances with God's will. It fosters unwavering belief in God's Word, affirming biblical truth despite skepticism. By creating a divine partnership, believers are connected to God's limitless power. It grants access to divine strength, transforming challenges into victories. The spirit of faith invites divine intervention, ensuring timely help and breakthroughs. It empowers believers to overcome worldly systems and adversities with confidence. Finally, it activates God's integrity to fulfill His promises, refining character through trials and ensuring His Word is accomplished.

As a believer, you carry the spirit of faith within you. Embrace it and walk boldly in its power, for the spirit of faith truly makes all the difference in the world.

Chapter Fifteen

The Mustard Seed Principle: Faith's Small Beginning

And the apostles said to the Lord, "Increase our faith."

— Luke 17:5

This request is fascinating because it likely stemmed from a discussion the disciples had among themselves, reflecting on all the miracles Jesus was performing and the consistent results He was getting. They must have realized that faith was the common denominator in all these events, prompting them to approach Jesus with this request.

It's noteworthy that they didn't ask Jesus to increase their compassion or love, even though those are important. They were captivated by the results Jesus was getting, and they identified faith as the key to those outcomes. They wanted more of *that* kind of faith. But faith isn't something that grows through physical effort or exercises like pushups; it operates differently, often unfolding in the invisible realm.

When they asked for more faith, Jesus pointed them to the mustard seed. He said, *"If you have faith as small as a mustard seed, you can say to this mulberry tree, 'Be uprooted and planted in the sea,' and it would obey you"* (Luke 17:6). This mustard seed faith, though tiny, holds immense potential. The mustard seed Jesus referred to in Israel was far smaller than the mustard seeds you might find in American seed packets—so small that it's almost invisible to the naked eye.

Yet, when planted, this tiny seed grows into a large bush or tree-like herb that birds can nest in. Jesus was conveying a powerful truth about the nature of faith. Genuine faith, even in its smallest form, is sufficient to accomplish great things. It's not about the size or quantity of faith; it's about the quality and the fact that it's the God-kind of faith.

This God-kind of faith isn't meant for creating entire galaxies or worlds; God has already done that. Instead, it's for creating and shaping the world we live in, our personal world. The faith within us, even as small as a mustard seed, is enough to get the job done, whatever that job may be in our lives.

This is reinforced when Jesus says, "Have faith in God," (Mark 11:22) or more literally, "Have the God-kind of faith." With even a mustard seed-sized amount of this faith, we can speak to obstacles in our lives—whether they are mulberry trees, mountains, or problems like debt or sickness—and command them to move, and they will obey.

This isn't just about praying for problems to go away; it's about using our God-given authority to speak directly to those problems and command them to leave. For example, if someone has been suffering from a recurring headache, they can use this faith to speak to the headache, commanding it to leave in Jesus' name.

The same principle applies to financial issues like credit card debt. By speaking to the debt and commanding it to be uprooted and removed—just as Jesus taught with the mulberry tree—we exercise our faith. However, faith is not a license to misuse credit or live beyond our means. Debt often reflects a lack of self-control, an area that requires intentional focus and growth. Recognizing this need is the first step toward change.

When you commit to walking in financial integrity, the journey begins by applying the faith you already possess. If God could handle the debt of our sins and provide for our redemption, how much more can He help bring you out of financial debt? Trust Him—He's more than capable of doing it.

While the exact process of how faith works may remain a mystery—much like how a seed grows in the ground—we know that it does work. The seed of faith, once planted and nurtured, will grow and produce results.

The apostles asked for increased faith, but Jesus showed them that they already had what they needed. It wasn't about the quantity of faith, but about using and cultivating the faith they already possessed, no matter how small. With that, they could accomplish what God had called them to do—and so can you!

Chapter Sixteen

Defying the Odds: Breaking Barriers and Achieving the Impossible

> And when they had come to the multitude, a man came to Him, kneeling down to Him and saying, "Lord, have mercy on my son, for he is an epileptic and suffers severely…"
>
> — Matthew 17:14-15

The term *epileptic* here is quite intriguing, as the original Greek word suggests that the boy was *moonstruck*. It's fascinating to think that there are times or seasons—perhaps certain phases of the moon or specific times of the year —when people seem to be more susceptible to strange behaviors. It's almost as if they become like automatons, easily manipulated by spiritual forces that seek expression through willing or vulnerable vessels.

In some cases, it's as if there's no one home, as though the person is merely a shell, and something else is trying to manifest through them. We see this kind of phenomenon at certain times, like Halloween or during politically charged seasons, when people seem to succumb to a spirit that drives them to act in ways that are completely out of character.

This brings to mind the "Jerusalem Syndrome," a documented phenomenon where visitors to Jerusalem—especially those who are spiritually immature—suddenly begin to behave in irrational or bizarre ways. I've witnessed this firsthand.

On one particular trip to Israel, I was invited as a guest speaker for a well-known television personality's tour. There were hundreds of people on the tour, but one man, in particular, caught everyone's attention. He had decided not to bring his medication with him, hoping that God would heal him during his time in Jerusalem.

Unfortunately, as his medication wore off, his condition worsened, and on the final day of the trip, he climbed up on the Temple Mount, took off his shirt, and began waving it around like a flag, shouting, "I'm ready to die a holy martyr!" He was ranting about jihad and other wild things. The Israeli police were understandably alarmed, but after some questioning, they realized he was just an American tourist whose medication had worn off. This is a prime example of how spirits can easily work through people who are spiritually weak or mentally unstable.

Returning to the story in the Book of Matthew, we see that this boy's condition was much more than a mere medical issue—it was the work of a demonic spirit. The boy would often fall into the fire or water, trying to harm or even kill himself. This is how we can discern whether something is of God or of the devil. If it were God's doing, He would gently place the boy on a couch or a chair. But because it was the work of the devil, the boy was thrown into dangerous situations, proving that the devil is always out to destroy.

The boy's father brought him to Jesus' disciples, but they couldn't heal him. Jesus' response was pointed: *"O faithless and perverse generation, how long shall I be with you? How long shall I bear with you? Bring him here to Me"* (Matthew 17:17). The real issues, He highlighted, were the lack of faith and the distorted nature of that generation.

For faith to work powerfully, it flows best from an open and honest heart. When we miss the mark or make a mistake, repentance is a gentle but essential way to stay close to God and keep our faith strong. Though the word *repentance* may feel challenging, it's simply a step that keeps our hearts aligned and our faith vibrant, enabling us to experience the fullness of God's love and power.

Jesus then rebuked the demon, and it came out of the boy immediately, curing him from that very hour. Some deliverances, healings, and miracles happen in an instant, while others unfold within a period of time. The anointing works within the individual, driving out the affliction and restoring them to wholeness.

Later, the disciples came to Jesus privately and asked, *"Why could we not cast it out?"* Jesus replied, *"Because of your unbelief"* (Matthew 17:19-20). There was still doubt lingering in their hearts. Jesus went on to explain that even faith as small as a mustard seed—a tiny but potent measure of the God-kind of faith—has the power to dispel doubts and remove mountains.

When you meditate on the Word of God, when you spend time in the Scriptures, even just a few verses can ignite your faith like a volcano ready to erupt. That's why it's important to pause and soak in those moments when the Word of God speaks directly to your spirit. It doesn't take a lot of faith—just a mustard seed-sized amount—to command mountains to move.

Jesus instructs us not just to pray about our mountains but to speak to them directly. When your faith is built up, when it's brimming with divine power, you'll find yourself making bold declarations. You'll say to this mountain, "Move from here to there," and it will move. Faith works, but you have to work your faith. When you do, it will produce the results you need.

This is something you need to stay focused on—whether you're chipping away at the mountain piece by piece or hitting it repeatedly until it suddenly slides away like an avalanche into the sea. Sometimes, the obstacle will disappear in an instant; other times, it will be removed gradually. But if you persist in faith, it will eventually move. Jesus said, *"Move from here to there, and it will move"* (Matthew 17:20). Now, let's take a moment to really absorb this. These are some of the most mind-boggling statements Jesus made. We might read them and think, "Wow, that's incredible," but we need to meditate on them and let them sink into our spirit. Jesus said, *"And nothing will be impossible for you."*

Think about that—nothing. There is no mountain in your life, no obstacle, no challenge, no barrier that represents something contrary to God's will that you cannot speak to in faith and command to move. Nothing will be impossible for you. There are things in your life that you need to speak to and command to leave. And there are other things, good things, that you need to call into your life—things that are part of your destiny. Speak to them and say, "Come on in! You're part of God's plan for me." Hallelujah!

You can be healed, but you must speak to that sickness or disease with strong, mustard-seed faith and command it to leave. Tell it to go, and it will. You can speak to abundance and say, "Come into my life!" You can speak to toxic debt and command it to move out of your life, throwing it into the sea in the name of Jesus. And it will obey you. Whatever God has put on your heart, you can achieve. Whether it's traveling abroad, attending a certain college, or pursuing a dream—nothing will be impossible for you if you operate in faith.

No believer should sit idly by and tolerate mountains in their lives. Every believer has a responsibility to do their part in moving those obstacles out of the way. In Matthew 17:19, the disciples asked Jesus privately, *"Why could we not cast it out?"* referring to the spirit of epilepsy that afflicted the child. But this principle applies to anything—whether it's casting out sickness, resolving a persistent problem, or overcoming an obstacle that's troubling you. Often, the root issue is unbelief. While we may have faith for salvation or for receiving the baptism in the Holy Spirit, certain challenges can be stubborn, clinging like a pestilence that refuses to leave. Yet, if you keep applying your faith, those obstacles will eventually dissolve and be removed.

Jesus said, *"However, this kind does not go out except by prayer and fasting"* (Matthew 17:21). Absolutely—there are some stubborn devils that won't respond to anything else. It doesn't matter how loud you scream or how fervently you shout, even if you're full of Pentecostal fire. If there's no anointing, the devil won't budge. In fact, he might even find it amusing, thinking you're just wearing yourself out. You must operate in the Spirit, staying vigilant and aware, especially when the enemy tries to strike at a low point in your life.

I have a rare book on my shelf in my personal library. It tells the story from about 70 years ago in South Africa involving a great man of God named William Duma. Pastor Duma was at a low point in his life, overwhelmed with ministry and lacking time for prayer. During this time, a visiting preacher from England requested to have his picture taken with a real witch doctor.

Although Duma was reluctant, he felt obligated to oblige. The next day, they encountered one of the leading witch doctors, who was completely demon-possessed. What started as a simple photo request quickly spiraled into a dangerous situation. The witch doctor lured them into his hut, where the atmosphere became oppressive, filled with the sound of hundreds of hissing snakes. The witch doctor declared that his ancestral spirits were present and that they would bind the souls of the two preachers.

In that moment, Pastor Duma, who was usually a spiritual giant, realized he had neglected his time with God and was spiritually unprepared for such a confrontation. It took everything he had to escape that situation and return to his place of prayer. He had to fast and pray for days just to break free from the dense spiritual fog and dark oppression that came over him. During that time, the enemy even tried to lure him into the ocean to drown him, but an angel intervened and saved him at the last moment.

This story highlights the importance of staying spiritually vigilant. There are stubborn cases and hard battles that require fasting and prayer. We must be on our guard, prepared to face whatever comes our way with the power and anointing of the Holy Spirit.

Let me give you another word of insight: some Christians go years—decades even—without ever fasting because they're waiting for some divine prompting. But fasting is a spiritual discipline. Jesus didn't say *if* you fast; He said *when* you fast. Just as we are called to give and pray, fasting is essential for spiritual vitality and health. So, even if you don't feel a special leading, make it a part of your regular spiritual practice. When you combine fasting with prayer and the Word, your faith will be fortified, and you will become a formidable force against the kingdom of darkness.

Always be mindful to pray daily, especially if you are involved in deliverance or spiritual warfare. The enemy is not pleased when you are on the frontlines, and he will try to attack when you are tired or vulnerable. After significant spiritual victories, it's important to stay grounded and humble.

After William Duma raised a girl from the dead through God's power—an event that sent shockwaves through the community and attracted attention in newspapers far and wide—Jesus appeared to him in a vision and said, "Duma, My servant, you sit down in the dust for the rest of your life. That which you have seen and heard was granted to you because of your great faith and humble spirit. Beware of pride, watch and pray, lest Satan destroy you with its poison."[1]

Remember, as you walk in faith and do what God has called you to do, you must also work with God's timing. Don't get frustrated or upset if things don't happen on your schedule. *"But as for me, I trust in You, O Lord; I say, 'You are my God.' My times are in Your hand"* (Psalm 31:14-15). Trust that your times are in God's hands. Turn off the countdown timer you've set on God, stop worrying about how old you are or how long it's taking, and walk in the Spirit.

Faith is always in the present—faith is always now. But manifestation happens in God's perfect timing. Don't let anyone, even well-

---

1. *Take Your Glory Lord by Mary Garnett. The Life Story of William Duma.* Copyright 2000, One Way Publications. Page 53.

meaning people, cause you to doubt God's timing. It's important to avoid the frustration or bitterness that can come from comparing your progress to others' expectations. God's timing is perfect, and He knows when you are truly ready for the breakthrough.

> He has made everything beautiful in its time...
>
> — Ecclesiastes 3:11

When the time is right, God will bring about beautiful results in your life. Trust Him, be patient, and stay in faith, knowing that His timing is always perfect.

> "And blessed is he who is not offended because of Me."
>
> — Matthew 11:6

Jesus spoke these words in response to John the Baptist's struggle as he sat in prison, rethinking his life and ministry.

Sadly, John was on the verge of losing his life, and it's clear he had begun to question his path. John's anointing was strong when he was in the wilderness, preaching repentance and baptizing people. That was his lane, where God had called him to be. However, as he observed the growing success of Jesus' ministry, John may have thought, "Perhaps I need to change my approach. Maybe I should move out of the wilderness and into the city, closer to the seats of power."

And so, John ventured out of his anointing, stepping into the political arena. Unfortunately, by doing so, he found himself in a situation that led to his imprisonment and, eventually, his execution.

John was a powerful voice in the wilderness, but when he tried to move into a space where he wasn't called, it led to his downfall.

Now, sitting in prison, John was discouraged and questioning everything. He sent his disciples to ask Jesus, *"Are You the Coming One, or do we look for another?"* (Matthew 11:3). It's clear that John was offended—offended that things hadn't turned out the way he expected, offended that he was in prison while the Messiah he had announced was free and thriving. Jesus' response was telling: *"Blessed is he who is not offended because of Me."*

This is a memorable warning for all of us. Don't let timing issues or unmet expectations lead you to become offended with God. You might be on the verge of the greatest breakthrough in your life, but if you allow offense to take root, you could miss the blessing God has in store for you. David said, *"I will bless the Lord at all times; His praise shall continually be in my mouth"* (Psalm 34:1). Some of us need to revisit that commitment—to bless the Lord at all times, regardless of our circumstances.

Setting time limits on God is a sign of spiritual immaturity, even spiritual foolishness. Instead, celebrate God's timing and follow Him closely. When the time is right, everything in your life will fall into place, and people will look at you and say, "Wow, that person has it all together." That's what God is doing for you. So, let Him do His work. Let Him make those last-minute adjustments so that when the blessing comes, you are fully prepared to receive it without making poor decisions that could cost you dearly.

Jesus said something very weighty in John 10:

> "Therefore My Father loves Me, because I lay down My life that I may take it again. No one takes it from Me, but I

> lay it down of Myself. I have power to lay it down, and I have power to take it again. This command I have received from My Father."
>
> —John 10:17-18

This passage isn't just a statement of Jesus' authority over His own life; it's also a revelation of what will be true for the end-time church. What does this mean? It means power over any form of untimely death. For those walking in the anointing as sons and daughters of God, there is literally power over death. If God calls you to preach in a dangerous place, even a place where your life could be at risk, you can go with confidence that you won't die before your time. If someone tries to take your life, God will have the power to raise you back up. Just as Paul was stoned and left for dead, only to rise up and continue his ministry, this power will be available to the church as we approach the return of Jesus.

You may need this anointing in the days ahead, especially if God calls you to minister in a hostile environment. The church is destined to walk in power—power over sickness, power over nature, and yes, power over death itself. This is the church Jesus will return for, a conquering, victorious church walking in the full authority of Christ. So, let's embrace this promise.

Let me introduce you to someone you'll one day meet in Heaven—a man known as Saint Denis. He's often depicted in church history holding his head in his hands, and I know what you're thinking: "Pastor Steven, why is he holding his head?" Well, that's because this is the famous Saint Denis, martyred for his faith, and now honored as the first Bishop of Paris. His story is as powerful as it is miraculous.

You see, back in the day, much of what is now modern-day France was under Roman control, steeped in paganism. Denis traveled from Italy with the express purpose of preaching the gospel to the pagans in Gaul, the ancient region of what is now France. He did an incredible job, starting churches, building an underground movement of believers, and even holding services in catacombs to avoid persecution. In fact, there's a place in Paris today where you can visit one of these very catacombs where he once held services.

However, as Denis continued his ministry, the Roman authorities eventually caught up with him. They demanded that he worship the emperor as a god, but Denis, of course, refused. They warned him that he would lose his head if he didn't comply, and he bravely told them to go ahead. So, they beheaded him, thinking they had silenced him for good.

But what happened next was nothing short of miraculous. After Denis was beheaded, his body reached down, picked up his head, and carried it in his hands. But he didn't just carry it—he walked for three miles, preaching the entire way! Can you imagine that? Preaching with your own severed head in your hands?

Saint Denis finally reached a spot where he decided, "This is the place I want to be buried." That spot is now marked by the Saint Denis Abbey Church, a beautiful country church just outside Paris. The city of Paris itself is built on the faith and backbone of this man's preaching. Today, you can still visit this church, and it's where nearly all of France's famous kings are buried—right next to the saint who fearlessly preached the gospel, even after death.

What a testimony! Denis called his shots under the anointing of the Holy Spirit, not the enemy. And this same anointing is coming upon the end-time church for those who are willing to receive it.

You can walk in this anointing, too, and preach fearlessly, whether you're in Pakistan, Los Angeles, Chicago, London, or anywhere else where people may not be happy about the Gospel message you're bringing. But if God is with you, no bullet, no sword, no opposition can stand against you.

Now, if you're doing this in the flesh, it won't end well. But if you're doing it in the Spirit, nothing can stop you. For those who feel this fire burning within them and are ready to receive this anointing, I invite you to lift your hands right now.

"Father, I pray for those who are reading this. For some, this is burning like a fire within them. I thank You that not only Saint Denis walked in this anointing, but many others throughout church history have as well—those who faced spears that couldn't penetrate, and fires that couldn't consume. They laughed in the face of danger and adversity, knowing that victory was theirs. Father, I thank You that the end-time church will know nothing but victory, carried on the wings of humility. And when we leave, we leave on terms of overcoming, in Jesus' name." Amen.

Chapter Seventeen

Faith Ascension: Insights to New Spiritual Realms

Let's delve into Hebrews 11:3, which offers rich insights into the nature of faith. The first key point is this: faith sees the invisible and brings it into manifestation. Notice the emphasis on seeing in verse 3: *"By faith, we understand that the worlds were framed by the Word of God so that the things which are seen were not made of things which are visible."* This is crucial. Everything we see today—the mountains, the oceans, the animals—was created from what is invisible. Faith, therefore, is the means by which the unseen becomes seen.

This concept is fascinating because it reveals that creation itself was birthed from the invisible. God saw what was hidden and brought it into existence. Faith operates in the same way; it sees the invisible and brings it to pass. We see this again in Hebrews 11, where it says of Moses, *"By faith, he forsook Egypt, not fearing the wrath of the king; for he endured as seeing Him who is invisible"* (Hebrews 11:27).

How, we might ask, does one see the invisible? The answer is through the spirit of faith.

This insight is crucial for making quantum leaps forward in our spiritual walk. To move into new levels supernaturally, we must use our faith to see what our physical eyes cannot. This means we must see our lives not as they are, but as we desire them to be, building our world just as God built His.

The second insight is that faith thinks the unthinkable. It contemplates possibilities that others might dismiss as impossible. Consider Abraham, the father of faith.

> And not being weak in faith, he did not consider his own body, already dead (since he was about a hundred years old), and the deadness of Sarah's womb. He did not waver at the promise of God through unbelief, but was strengthened in faith, giving glory to God.
>
> — Romans 4:19-20

The phrase *"he did not consider"* suggests that Abraham refused to allow his mind to dwell on the apparent impossibility of God's promise.

Faith, therefore, enables us to think the unthinkable. Abraham did not allow logic or the apparent reality to dictate his belief. He wasn't in denial of the facts; he simply didn't let them override his faith. True biblical faith, as we know, is not of the intellect but of the heart. Natural conditions and negative circumstances have no sway over a person operating under the spirit of faith.

Some might not understand this approach, but the results that Abraham experienced speak for themselves—just look at Isaac, the child of promise. Jesus said that wisdom is justified by its children, and in the same way, the wisdom of God's Word, when applied in faith, produces undeniable results. Those who can't grasp it often struggle because they are not engaging with their hearts, where true faith resides.

Many Christians live governed entirely by their five physical senses. Some do develop their minds, an area that can be expanded and enriched throughout one's life. After all, brain cells can be renewed, and there's always something new to learn. However, the spiritual realm requires a different connection—one made with the heart, because you are a spirit, and you have a soul.

Your soul encompasses your mind, intellect, and emotions, and of course, you live in a physical body. But it is the spirit of a person—the heart—that embarks on the faith journey. This faith walk will take you further than intellect ever can, propelling you beyond what is unthinkable to the natural mind.

Consider Abraham. He did not ponder his own body's limitations or write out reasons why God's promise couldn't happen. Instead, he thought the unthinkable, firmly believing he would have a child because God had promised it. And, astonishingly, Isaac was born. These types of miracles continue today through the expression of true biblical faith. Such faith can catapult you from barrenness or dry seasons into explosive growth and blessing, simply by understanding these insights.

The third insight is that faith expects the unexpected, even when others are pessimistic. Some people, even within the church, can cloak their doubt and unbelief in religious language. But this didn't work in ancient Israel, and it won't work today. Miracles come not by heritage or lineage but by faith and trust in God.

Faith expects what seems impossible. A prime example of this is found in 2 Kings 7, where the prophet Elisha declares, *"Tomorrow, about this time, a seah of fine flour will sell for a shekel, and two seahs of barley for a shekel, at the gate of Samaria"* (2 Kings 7:1). In the midst of a severe famine, this seemed utterly implausible, comparable to predicting that gasoline would suddenly drop to 5 cents a gallon. Yet, Elisha was speaking the Word of the Lord, and it was going to happen.

However, the king's officer, full of doubt, retorted, *"Look, even if the Lord made windows in heaven, could this thing be?"* Elisha responded, *"You shall see it with your eyes, but you shall not eat of it"* (2 Kings 7:2). His doubt cost him dearly. Faithless people like the king's officer cannot expect the unexpected, even when a great prophet delivers a promise from God.

We, however, must expect the unexpected. Expect God to break out in abundance, even in times of famine. Whether it's gasoline, groceries, pet supplies, or a job—have an expectancy that God can meet your needs.

This is how we leap to extraordinary levels of blessing and empowerment. Real faith brings about experiences that others simply cannot comprehend. There are mysteries within the Kingdom of God, and since faith is a core principle of that Kingdom, it often manifests in ways that defy logic and reason. These manifestations puzzle onlookers, as they witness you thriving in times when it seems impossible. God delights in validating His Word during difficult times, proving that He can move in any situation, at any time, day or night.

The fourth insight to supernaturally shifting to new levels is that faith conquers the unconquerable. You might be thinking, "Pastor Steven, we don't have a chance. We're outnumbered. The odds are against us." But we've seen this scenario before in the Bible, and we know that when people turn to the Lord and put their trust in Him, God delights in responding in unusual and mighty ways.

One of the greatest examples of this truth is found in the story of Gideon and his army of 300 men. Gideon started with 32,000 soldiers, but God told him, "You've got too many." If Gideon had gone into battle with that many men, they might have been tempted to take the glory for themselves. God wanted to make it clear that the victory would be His, so He had Gideon reduce his army until only 300 men remained.

Now, Gideon and his 300 men were up against an army of 135,000 trained soldiers—a ratio of 450 to 1. It's as if each of Gideon's men was responsible for defeating 450 enemies. In the natural, this seemed impossible. But Gideon trusted God, and with that trust, they went into battle and achieved a miraculous victory.

This is why the Book of Hebrews says, *"Who through faith subdued kingdoms, worked righteousness, obtained promises, stopped the mouths of lions"* (Hebrews 11:33). This verse gives a flashback to Gideon's victory, highlighting that through faith, the unconquerable was conquered.

When it's you and God, and you are fully leaning on Him, your team is undefeatable. Faith conquers the unconquerable, and it can certainly take you to new levels, just as it did for Gideon. He went from being an outcast to becoming the judge of Israel, all because of the faith he placed in God.

Moving on to the next insight, number five: Faith achieves the unachievable.

This is a realm where the Holy Spirit wants to break you into—into a place where you've been told you could never achieve. Maybe people have said, "You don't belong in that realm; you weren't made for that." But God not only takes you toward it, He can take you into it, cause you to stand in it, and achieve even what others would say is unachievable.

One of the great examples of this is found in the story of Ezra. In Ezra 3:11, we read about the Israelites who sang and praised the Lord because the foundation of the Lord's house was laid. Originally, Moses had a Tabernacle, which later transitioned into the temple built by Solomon. However, that temple was destroyed, and now, in Ezra's time, they were rebuilding the second temple.

It took two years to clear and level the ruins, to haul away the rubble left from the Babylonian destruction, and to lay the foundation of the temple. Zerubbabel, the governor of Jerusalem and head of the tribe of Judah, led this effort.

But then, for 17 years, the work came to a complete halt due to intense opposition and persecution. The Samaritans stirred up trouble, falsely offered help, and frustrated the work with red tape, lies, and threats. It seemed like the unachievable was truly unachievable.

Yet, God raised up prophets like Haggai and Zechariah, who prophesied and reignited the hearts of God's people. After a 17-year delay, they re-engaged in the work, and in just four years, they completed the rebuilding of the temple.

This story shows that faith achieves the unachievable. When you lean into your calling with all your heart, God will send the resources, the provision, the skilled laborers—whatever you need to accomplish what He has set before you. It may not be the rebuilding of a physical temple, but whatever it is that God has called you to do, you can accomplish it through faith. What may seem unachievable in the natural is entirely achievable through faith.

So, lift your hands and declare, "With God's help, I can do it." Let the Spirit of God encourage you. And though we don't have Zechariah and Haggai here to prophesy to you in person, God will bring the support and the word you need in one way or another. All of Heaven is backing you.

And by the way, if you find yourself in need of laughter and joy—perhaps you've grown a bit weary along the way—God knows how to bring that to you too. If there's anyone who knows how to catch you off guard with the most unexpected, hilarious, and wonderful statements, it's the Holy Spirit.

Oh, Pastor Steven, some might say, "Everything with God must be serious." Yes, we approach God with reverence and respect. But let me tell you, there's no one like the Holy Spirit when it comes to bringing joy into your life. He has a way of saying things so unexpectedly—sometimes with a clever pun or a playful double meaning—that you can't help but laugh. And sometimes, the humor is so simple and light-hearted that all you can do is smile and say, "God, there's truly nobody like You."

Remember, the Holy Spirit is not a force, a cloud, a dove, or a fire. He's not wind or any other impersonal element. He is a person—the third person of the Godhead. He can manifest His presence in these various forms, but at His core, He is a person. And even if we can't have Zechariah or Haggai come and prophesy to you, the Holy Spirit Himself is with you. He can speak a word to you, no matter where you are, that will lift your spirit, make you laugh, and get you right back on track, fully engaged in your own *temple-building* project.

You see, the temple in Ezra's time took a little longer to complete due to various setbacks, but in the end, it was finished. That same temple—though later expanded and adorned by Herod—was the very temple Jesus walked into. When it was first rebuilt, the older generation wept because they remembered the former glory of Solomon's temple. They didn't realize that the prophecy declared that the latter glory would be even greater than the former. They couldn't comprehend that this was the temple the Messiah would enter, which is why some of them wept. If they had understood that the Christ would walk into this very temple, their tears would have turned into joy.

So, my friend, we need to take God's words by faith and believe that He always has our best interests at heart. These principles of faith are not just for historical figures—they're for us today. They are tools we can use to accomplish things the world says can't be done.

But let's ask ourselves: How does faith get these impossible things done? The answer is straightforward. We accomplish these great things by drawing on the power of God. When we tap into His power, nothing is truly impossible, and what seems unachievable becomes within reach.

Chapter Eighteen

Forceful Faith: Seizing What Belongs to You

Let me take you to the New Testament to show you an example of forceful faith, found in the Gospel of Mark. Of the four Gospels, Mark happens to be my favorite. We're going to focus on a story in Mark 5, starting in verse 25, about the woman with the issue of blood.

To begin with, understand that in Jewish culture, according to Mosaic law, this woman was considered unclean due to her condition. This meant she couldn't work, because her condition would prevent her from socially interacting with others. This undoubtedly affected her finances and left her isolated, unable to participate in the feast days. Essentially, she was cut off from the community and treated as an outcast because of her physical affliction. The mental and emotional toll of such isolation must have been immense, likely leading to depression and despondency.

In verse 26, it tells us that this woman had suffered many things from many physicians. Imagine the humiliation and embarrassment she endured as male doctors repeatedly examined her, only to leave her condition unresolved and her dignity in shreds. She had spent all her money on treatments, but instead of getting better, her condition only worsened.

Then, verse 27 tells us something crucial: *"When she heard about Jesus..."* We know that faith comes by hearing, but it's not just hearing about a nice man or a kind teacher. No, she heard about the miracles and the power of God at work in His life and ministry. When you start hearing testimonies of others receiving their miracles, something inside you begins to rise. You start to think, *"If others are getting their miracle, I can receive mine too."* And when you're desperate, when all other options have failed, faith within you comes alive when you hear what God is doing in the lives of others. That's the challenge for many in the Western Church today. We have so many options that we can almost cruise through life without really exercising our faith. Just get a good-paying job, eat healthy, exercise, and trust God—but not in a way that truly stretches your faith.

But let me tell you, life has a way of throwing curveballs. The devil can bring something into your life that challenges you to your core, and suddenly, you realize, "I'm out of shape spiritually. I haven't been exercising my faith, and now I'm struggling to deal with this situation." Even in the natural realm, no amount of wealth or success can shield you from certain challenges. Remember Steve Jobs, one of the richest men in the world, the man who made Apple a global phenomenon? Yet, when he got sick, all the money and the best doctors in the world couldn't save him. He died at the age of 56.

These moments remind us of Jesus' words in Luke 18:8, where He asks, *"When the Son of Man comes, will He really find faith on the earth?"* We live in a time where options and conveniences are abundant. But you can't enter your destiny zone on "nice." The violent—those with forceful, persistent faith—take it by force. You can't cruise into the levels God wants you to step into; it requires a violent, aggressive faith. This is one of the greatest challenges for the modern Church, not just in the Western world but globally.

Jesus rebuked the Laodicean church in the Book of Revelation, but He also gave them a special promise. He said, *"If you overcome, you will sit with Me on My throne, just as I overcame and sat with My Father on His throne"* (Revelation 3:21). The only way to overcome is by walking the faith walk, maintaining it even when it's easy to settle for comfort. The promises are rich, especially for those who overcome in times of prosperity. It's one thing to trust God in persecution and poverty, but it's another thing entirely to cling to Him in the midst of abundance, when the world says, "Why do you even need God?"

Back to our story in Mark: when the woman heard about Jesus, she came up behind Him in the crowd and touched His garment. For she said, *"If only I may touch His clothes, I shall be made well"* (Mark 5:28). Now, let's pay close attention to what happens next. Immediately, the fountain of her blood was dried up, and she felt in her body that she was healed of the affliction. Jesus, knowing that power had gone out of Him, turned around and asked, *"Who touched My clothes?"* His disciples, not understanding, said, *"You see the multitude thronging You, and You say, 'Who touched Me?'"* (Mark 5:29-31). But Jesus knew—He knew that someone had drawn power from Him through faith.

This is what faith does. It connects you to God in a way that releases His power into your life. This is not just about believing in God; it's about making a connection with Him that pulls power from Heaven into your situation. And you can't get there without that power. When Jesus said, *"Who touched Me?"* He was essentially saying, "Someone just pulled power out of Me." That's the power of the Spirit riding on Him with a mighty anointing. And that's what the woman's faith did—it made a connection with God that drew His power into her life.

When you connect with God by faith, you're drawing from a failure-proof source. This is why you can trust God completely. It wasn't the physical touch that healed the woman; it was her touch of faith. Many people bumped into Jesus, curious onlookers touching Him, but nothing happened to them because they weren't touching Him with faith.

Faith isn't just about believing; it's about connecting. And when you make that connection, power flows. That power puts you in control, breaking the chains that have bound you, just as it did for this woman. No longer was she under the oppression of a demonic work; she was now free. When faith connects you to God, it positions you to be in control. So, keep reaching out in faith, keep pulling on God, and you will receive a power jolt that will catapult you to a significantly higher level.

This is the kind of faith that Abraham, David, Ezra, Nehemiah, and the great prophets like Elijah and Elisha demonstrated. They were people of faith, but they also made that crucial connection with God. My friend, keep reaching, keep pulling, and you're going to receive a powerful testimony that will glorify God.

Chapter Nineteen

New Beginnings: How Faith Can Rewrite Your Story

Jesus speaks these powerful words: *"Therefore, whatever they tell you, do and comply with it all, but do not do as they do, for they say things and do not do them"* (Matthew 23:3 NASB). What a profound statement. They say things but do not do them.

Over the past few weeks, I've encountered people who have been disappointed by broken promises from fellow Christians—people who promised to help but then backed out when the time came. It's disheartening when someone's word is not kept, and I've had to explain to these individuals that, unfortunately, this happens. It's wrong, but we must forgive, move on, and trust that God will bless us despite the failings of others.

The Bible tells us that God exalts His Word above His own name, so if our word is no good, then our name is no good either. We are called to keep our word, even if it costs us something. As Scripture says, *"He keeps his word even to his own disadvantage and does not change it [for his own benefit]"* (Psalm 15:4 AMP). When we do this, we become more careful not to overcommit. We begin to pause, reflect, and ensure that we can follow through on what we say before making any promises.

The Pharisees, however, didn't operate that way. They were quick to say things without any intention of doing them. They expected others to comply with their words, yet they themselves had no intention of practicing what they preached. This is why some modern paraphrased translations say, *"They do not practice what they preach."* They were full of talk but lacked the follow-through.

In the realm of faith, what we say must align with what we do. I've had people tell me, "Pastor Steven, over the years, we've seen many come into the local Christian community, declaring grand plans and intentions, but you're one of the few who actually does what you say." Many others had great ideas and visions, but they didn't follow through, leaving those promises unfulfilled. We must be careful in this area. Matthew 23:3 warns us against being like those who say things but do not do them.

This lesson is crucial because there's always something we can do to move our faith projects forward. Often, people want to skip phases or cut corners in their excitement to see the final outcome. However, each phase of a project has its purpose, and we must focus our faith on completing every phase with excellence. God often releases provision in phases, and when we diligently complete each phase, we're prepared for the next. The provision that God releases is secure, coming directly from the treasury of Heaven, and when it is released in sequence, it remains protected and cannot be stolen.

So, what should we do? Give full attention to where you are right now. Imagine you're on the board of directors for a Fortune 100 company. Each year, during the annual shareholders meeting, the directors strategize on how to increase profit, even if the previous year was exceptional. Excellence is always progressive, and the same applies to our faith. There's always room for growth, and we must fully apply ourselves to get the maximum results.

In the Western world, where comforts and distractions abound, it's easy to fall into the trap of cruising through life, expecting God to deliver extraordinary results with minimal input from us. But if you want to rise to the top, you must give it your all. We cannot be like the religious leaders of Jesus' time, who talked a good game but had no intention of following through. Faith is not just talking; faith is action.

The renowned British evangelist Smith Wigglesworth, known as an apostle of faith, often emphasized this point. An apostle, in the New Testament Greek language, means a *sent one,* and Wigglesworth carried a special message of faith to the body of Christ. He would run across the platform during his meetings, declaring to the audience, "Faith is an act." He repeated this over and over, trying to instill in people the understanding that faith is not merely believing in an abstract sense—it's taking action.

Consider the farmer during harvest season. If he has a bumper crop but decides he's only going to work eight hours a day because that's his limit, he'll end up leaving much of the harvest in the field to rot. Harvesting requires long hours and hard work. Similarly, our faith must be put into action if we want to see results.

So, let's not be like the religious leaders of Jesus' time, who were all talk and no action. We are called to live out our faith, to put our words into practice, and to see God's promises fulfilled in our lives.

Let's go to the Book of James, where this concept comes into full clarity. We'll focus on James chapter two, starting in verse 14. This passage reveals the implications of faith in action—faith that's truly released in your life.

"What does it profit, my brethren, if someone says he has faith but does not have works? Can faith save him?" (James 2:14). This is a powerful question, and it's one that we still encounter in the church today. There are people who claim to have faith—faith in God, faith for something beneficial to happen in their lives. But the reality is that they lack the works to back up that faith. Can such faith save them? The answer is no. Faith requires corresponding actions.

Years ago, I ministered at a church where, after my teaching session, the pastor asked the entire congregation to line up so that I could lay hands on them and minister prophetically as the Holy Spirit led. People came forward, and I prayed for everyone—healing for some and prophetic words for others. It took over an hour to minister to the 500 or 600 people there, but I moved quickly, ensuring that I laid hands on each person.

A year later, I returned to the same church to minister again. After the service, I went back to the pastor's office, where he was waiting with an elder and a woman who was a church member and had been in the previous meeting. As I walked in, it felt like a setup. The pastor, with a serious tone, said, "Brother Steven, we need to talk about a situation." I asked what the issue was, and he explained that the woman had claimed I had prophesied she would get married within a year and that it hadn't happened. She was upset, and they were looking to me for an explanation.

I was taken aback because I didn't recall giving any such prophecy. It's not my style to promise specific outcomes like marriage, especially within a set timeframe. I told the pastor, "I don't believe I said that." But the pastor insisted, pointing out that a tape recording was made during the service. I immediately suggested, "Let's play the tape and listen together."

Why they hadn't done this before confronting me was beyond me, but they agreed. The elder retrieved the tape—a cassette tape, mind you, from years ago, when cassette tapes were already outdated. We listened, and as it played, it became clear that I had not given any such prophecy. There was no mention of a timeline or a promise of marriage. The pastor turned to the woman and said, "Well, sister, it's not quite like you said, is it?" She begrudgingly agreed, but she was still upset.

Even though I was vindicated, the pastor and elder still emotionally sided with her. She was like a spiritual daughter to the pastor, and despite the evidence, their frustration was directed at me. It wasn't a pleasant experience, but I left the church knowing I had done nothing wrong.

Two weeks later, I had an extraordinary face-to-face vision of the Lord Jesus Christ. He appeared to me and brought up the situation with the woman. Jesus said to me, "She says she has faith for a husband. But if she does, why doesn't she wear a nice perfume?" Can you grasp the significance of this? Jesus, in His wisdom, pointed out the practical, everyday actions—or the lack thereof—that revealed her true level of faith.

And He wasn't done yet. He continued, "She says she has faith to get married, yet she dresses like a woman who wants to be a nun and join a convent." He wasn't joking or smiling when He said this; He was completely serious. It became clear that while she claimed to desire marriage, her appearance and attire told a different story.

She could have presented herself attractively, but her worn-out jeans, unattractive shoes, and drab colors made her look like someone who wasn't interested in a relationship. Jesus was revealing the disconnect between her claimed faith and how she actually lived.

When I shared this story, people often asked if I had gone back to tell the woman and the pastor what Jesus said. My answer is always "No." They wouldn't have received it. Jesus appeared to me for my benefit, not theirs. The purpose of this encounter was to free me from any sense of false guilt or responsibility that they had tried to project onto me for their own shortcomings.

Secondly, they had a skewed understanding of Jesus. They didn't grasp that you cannot please Him without faith—a subject they weren't interested in exploring. Many people expect sympathy instead of truth. They want Jesus to comfort them without addressing the root of their issues. But we must remember that after His resurrection, Jesus rebuked even His own disciples for their unbelief.

> Later He appeared to the eleven as they sat at the table; and He rebuked their unbelief and hardness of heart, because they did not believe those who had seen Him after He had risen.
>
> — Mark 16:14

This is a side of Jesus we must also embrace: true faith demands works—actions that align with what you claim to believe. Without these, your faith is dead—just empty religious talk with no power to bring real change.

The reality is that faith without works is lifeless. It's not enough to say you believe; you must act on that belief. The Western world, with all its comforts and distractions, can make it easy for people to fall into complacency. But if you want to see results, if you want to rise to the top, you must put in the work. Don't be like the religious leaders of Jesus' time, who talked a lot but did nothing. True faith is lived out in action.

This is not about being harsh; it's about being real. If you want to see God move in your life, align your actions with your faith and watch as He brings His promises to pass.

If you want to rise to the top and accomplish powerful things that bring great glory and honor to God, there will be moments when it's not just about believing—you've got to put in the work. And sometimes, that work can be extremely demanding. You might not get as much sleep as you want. You might think, "Why is so much being squeezed out of me?" But those who continually break through barriers and go higher know that pushing through is part of the process. Praise God, praise God!

So, how do you do it? Simply by putting works to your faith. Sometimes, it's as straightforward as taking a small action. For example, in the case of women who want to get married, think about it—how complicated or difficult is it to go out and buy a $45 bottle of perfume? God isn't asking you to fly to Paris and spend $2,000 on a half-ounce of perfume. He's just asking you to take a simple step, like going to the mall or ordering online to buy something modest, yet impactful.

There's a way of dressing and presenting yourself with excellence that makes a difference. You can have your hair done nicely, get your nails done, wear a nice perfume, and suddenly, things start to happen. Men who are single and potentially interested will start noticing, asking for your phone number, or even inquiring with the pastor about your availability. These simple actions send a message—you're someone who has your act together and is ready for more responsibility.

What does it profit if someone says they have faith but does not have works? The answer is clear: it profits nothing. Faith without works is dead. I think sometimes people separate faith from practical application, forgetting that there's always something they can go out and do to move forward.

If you're a single man wanting to get married, clean your car inside and out, use mouthwash, and put on a nice men's cologne. Don't make it too strong, but find a scent that's just right. If you're not sure how to do that, read up on it. Presenting yourself well conveys a message that you're stable and ready for more responsibility in life.

Now, let's look at the Book of James in the Amplified Bible. It's so good!

> If a brother or sister is poorly clad and lacks food for each day,
> And one of you says to him, Good-bye! Keep [yourself] warm and well fed, without giving him the necessities for the body, what good does that do?
> So also faith, if it does not have works (deeds and actions of obedience to back it up), by itself is destitute of power (inoperative, dead).
>
> —James 2:15-17 (AMPC)

This is what real faith looks like—faith in action. As James says, "Faith by itself, if it does not have works, is dead." Someone might say, "You have faith, and I have works," but I'll show you my faith by my works (James 2:17-18). Faith is meant to be active, not passive.

James then gives us two incredible examples of faith in action: Abraham and Rahab. Abraham's faith was made perfect by his works—when he was willing to offer Isaac on the altar, his faith wasn't just belief; it was action. He walked, gathered wood, built the altar, and prepared to sacrifice his son, trusting God completely.

There's something you can do right now to move your faith project forward. The money will come in increasing amounts as the works are being done, but the groundwork needs to be laid first. Preparatory work must be completed before the next release phase can manifest. Your faith is made perfect by your works, and whatever God has called you to do, your actions will bring it to completion.

It's time to put your faith into action and watch God bring His promises to pass in your life. Some have a desire to start a business. You have faith for it, but remember, faith alone isn't enough—you have to be willing to put in the work. It's not just about believing; it's about taking action.

Some might say, "Well, Pastor Steven, I'm on board as long as it doesn't demand more than eight hours a day, as long as I can still fit in all these other things." But the truth is, you've got to be willing to dive in fully, sometimes putting in twelve or sixteen-hour workdays or more. Without the effort, it's simply not going to get done. You have to pursue it with everything you've got.

As Scripture says, *"By works, faith was made perfect"* (James 2:22). So don't be afraid of the work. There is dignity in labor, and that's something we must embrace. We're seeing a generation today that leans heavily on entitlement, expecting everything to be handed to them. But if you haven't worked for something, you're not entitled to it. And here's the truth: if it's given to you for free, you'll never truly value or appreciate it. Praise God.

There's great dignity and honor in work. Thank you, Jesus. The Scripture was fulfilled, which says, "Abraham believed God, and it was accounted to him for righteousness." And he was called the friend of God (James 2:23).

In our pursuit of a deeper relationship with God, it's not just about how much we pray or even how much we fast, although those are important. What really brings us into that close, intimate walk with God is working on a faith frequency with Him—understanding what pleases Him and what grieves Him. What pleases God is when we believe Him, and what displeases Him is when we doubt Him.

> You see then that a man is justified by works, and not by faith only.
>
> —James 2:24

Here's another example: Rahab the harlot. This is remarkable—she made it into the *hall of faith* in Hebrews chapter 11, standing shoulder to shoulder with some of the greatest names in the Bible, like Moses. Her actions demonstrated her faith, and because of that, she secured a place in history. You can also achieve an incredible testimony!

Rahab's story shows us that no matter who you are or where you've come from, faith can rewrite your story. Rahab was a harlot, a total heathen by all accounts, yet she put her faith in God. She heard the reports about how God delivered the Israelites, parting the Red Sea and giving them victory over their enemies. She believed in the God of Israel, and her faith led to her deliverance when the city of Jericho was destroyed. Not only did God save her, but He also grafted her into the lineage of Israel. She married a man from the tribe of Judah, and from her lineage came King David and, ultimately, Jesus the Messiah. There's something about faith that allows you to rewrite your story.

When you're born-again and come into Christ Jesus, your story is rewritten. You are transferred out of the kingdom of darkness into the Kingdom of light. And as you walk in faith, God's promises are unveiled to you, and you can create something beautiful with your life that glorifies Him.

All of our works need to be done in faith. Don't rush into something out of fear or pressure. Take the time to build up your faith, ensure that God is in it, and then step forward with confidence. When faith is the root, the good works will follow as the fruit, proving that your faith is genuine.

Let's turn to the Book of Hebrews for a moment.

> By faith the walls of Jericho fell down after they were encircled for seven days. By faith the harlot Rahab did not perish with those who did not believe…
>
> — Hebrews 11:30-31

Rahab's faith tied her into the covenant of protection and blessing. While everyone else around her perished in unbelief, Rahab and her family were spared. Faith exempts you from being a statistic of calamity.

Some might say, "Well, Pastor Steven, you never know when disaster might strike—tornadoes, hurricanes, earthquakes—you just never know when your time may come." But I'm here to tell you that your time isn't coming until you've lived out your full life and accomplished everything God has called you to do. And until then, you're not going anywhere, and neither was Rahab. Her faith exempted her from the destruction that befell the unbelievers around her.

Recently, a tornado passed right by our church, just a few hundred yards away. It was a fierce storm, with the wind blowing so hard that the rain was coming down sideways. I was there when this took place. My wife, Kelly, called me and said, "Steven, they're reporting a tornado on the ground nearby. Are you in the bathroom where it's safest?" I replied, "No, I'm standing right here by the window, because if that tornado shows up here, I'm walking out there and talking to it." Praise God. This building has stood since 1877, and it's not going anywhere now. If anything tries to change that, we'll deal with it through the gift of special faith and speak to the storm as needed.

You can rewrite your story from tragedy to triumph, from being a victim to being victorious. You can rewrite it through faith. And as I stand here today, everything is fine. Not a shingle flew off; not a piece of metal was ripped off the roof. The storm passed, and the next thing you know, the sun was shining, and the skies were blue.

Was the tornado destructive in other areas? Yes, it was. But no one lost their life, and no one was injured. Praise God. You have to put your faith on the line, and when you do, you'll see the goodness of God in every situation.

Remember, faith is the root, but the works are the fruit. Let your actions reflect your faith, and watch as God's promises come to life in your world. I know the Holy Spirit is at work right now, stirring your hearts and minds. Even by faith, look for those areas where you can take the next step. Yes, you're aiming for the overall completion of a project, but remember, every project is accomplished in phases. Whether it's your business, your ministry, or even something as simple as building a garden in your backyard, there's always something you can do in the phase you're in right now.

Don't try to jump to the end. Yes, you can visualize the end—that's when the vision will speak—but right now, pour everything you've got into what you're doing. Don't skip phases. Do it the right way, and that takes discipline. But when you do things the right way, you're setting yourself up for lasting success.

As you move forward, phase by phase, God releases the provision you need. Many of you have dreams, and I want to ask you a simple question: Does the dream God has given you require money? For 95 percent of you, the answer is yes. But don't worry—God is going to release that provision to you.

You might say, "Pastor Steven, it hasn't happened yet." That just means there's something else you need to be preparing or doing before the next phase of release comes. You're making a heavenly withdrawal by faith from God's unending reserves, and He's going to get that provision to you. It often comes through people, opportunities, and divine doors that God opens. But until then, do everything you can in the now, before the next release comes. There's always something to do. Stay busy, stay engaged.

In the Gospel of Luke, Jesus talks about speaking to the mulberry tree and telling it to be thrown into the sea. Then, He immediately transitions into a farming analogy, saying that no man tells his servant to sit down and take a break. Instead, you keep that servant working while you eat. Jesus is making a point—keep your faith on the line, and remember that faith has works.

God will show you the next step. I want to help those who, unless they catch this revelation, will find themselves still talking year after year without seeing any results. It's not enough to talk—you have to be willing to put in the work. When God gives you an opportunity, you have to capitalize on it, even if it means going overtime.

"Heavenly Father, I pray for those who are reading this right now. I pray that Your Holy Spirit shows them what they can do in the present moment to check off a faith work that aligns with their belief. Father, we thank You. We give You praise that Your Holy Spirit is helping us, and we thank You that we will not stand before You empty-handed, but with a harvest of fruit for Your glory.

"We thank You for the gift of life—that life is not a grind, but a gift, and we embrace it with joy and the vitality that You supply. Father, thank You, in Jesus' name. Amen."

Chapter Twenty

Speak Life: How Your Words Direct Your Future

In the Book of Romans, we find this profound spiritual truth:

> For with the heart one believes unto righteousness, and with the mouth confession is made unto salvation.
>
> — Romans 10:10

This is nothing short of fascinating. It shows us that what we believe internally in our hearts must be spoken outwardly with our mouths, activating what is known as the creative force of faith. Faith, by its very nature, is inherently creative, dynamic, and powerful.

This is the divine, biblical method by which we receive salvation—eternal life in Christ Jesus. The Scriptures promise, "Whoever calls upon the name of the Lord shall be saved" (Romans 10:13). It's not just a hope or a suggestion; it is a promise, an assurance that when we believe in our hearts and call upon His name, salvation is guaranteed. Many of us have walked this very path—we have believed, we have called upon Him, and God, being ever faithful, has responded by saving us and bringing us into His family. We are now born again, sons and daughters of the Most High. But it's crucial to remember that this journey began with speaking from the heart.

This principle doesn't end at salvation—it's a divine law that applies across the board. In the same way that you used your mouth to make a confession unto salvation, bringing eternal life into your spirit and forgiveness of sins, this is not a one-time application. It's not as though we should say, "Well, that was great; now I'm saved, and that's it." No, this principle of faith, spoken from the heart, applies to every other area of life where we seek victory, deliverance, healing, provision, or breakthrough. The same faith that brought eternal life into your spirit can also bring transformation to your circumstances, relationships, finances, health, and every other facet of life. The key is learning to use your words in faith, repeatedly and consistently, to see victory in these areas.

Sadly, many people miss this. They used their mouth once to receive Christ—the greatest gift of all—but then fail to realize that they can and should continue using their words to release God's creative power in every part of their lives. God's Word is alive, and when spoken from a heart of faith, it brings about supernatural change. Just as you used your confession to receive Christ, you can use it to receive God's power, healing, provision, and deliverance in other areas. Your life can be beautiful, a reflection of the divine purpose and blessings God has in store for you. But it starts with understanding that your words are a creative force, and when combined with heartfelt belief, they shape the world around you.

Now, when we speak the Word, it must come from a place of deep conviction, from our hearts—not from our intellect, not from mere memorization, not from emotion, but from a heart that has meditated on the truth of God's Word. This requires laboring in the Word—not just to gain mental knowledge or to memorize verses, but to truly understand the heart of God in specific passages. The goal is not to gather a vast, encyclopedic knowledge of Scripture. While it is good to know many scriptures, the most important thing is to have a deep understanding of the Word that speaks directly to your situation.

Think about this: children are often taught to memorize Bible verses, perhaps at home or in Christian schools. They come home excited and say, "Mom, Dad, I learned this verse!" and they recite it, and parents are pleased. But here's the reality—memorizing a verse is good, but if that child doesn't know what it means, the verse remains just words. It has no power because the understanding is missing. And this is true for all of us: it's not enough to simply know Scripture by memorization; we must understand its meaning deeply and let it dwell in our hearts.

We're not talking about being a mile wide and an inch deep. Instead, we must go deep in the areas where we need victory. We must gain concentrated depth in selective scriptures—those that speak to our situation, those that hold the key to our breakthrough. And when we understand these scriptures and speak them with faith, they are the ones that work powerfully in our lives. Hallelujah!

It's the scriptures that you understand and declare with conviction that will bring results in your life. You can technically speak the truth, but if it only comes from your head and not from a heart filled with faith, the results you are seeking—victory, breakthrough, healing—may not materialize. This is the key that many believers miss. They wonder why they're not seeing the results of their faith, but the missing link is often that the Word has not moved from their heads to their hearts. It's only when the Word of God takes root in your heart that it produces the results you desire. This understanding must come alive within you.

I've learned that the Word of God is like precious gold and hidden gems. It's only those golden nuggets of truth, those specific, life-giving scriptures that make their way into your heart after you've labored in the Word, that produce the deep convictions necessary for victorious living. You don't need to memorize entire books of the Bible to experience victory—though that's a blessing if you can—but you must meditate on the scriptures that speak life into your situation. These truths will bypass your intellect and settle in your heart, where they become your convictions, the foundation of how you live and walk in victory.

It's those golden nuggets, those precious gems of revelation, that transform your life. It is not just a collection of knowledge but also a deep, heart-rooted truth that guides your actions and shapes your faith. This is what brings the results you're looking for—not just head knowledge or quoting scriptures, but truly believing in your heart and speaking in faith.

In today's world, there are many voices and teachings, but it's crucial to focus on those that lead you deeper into God's Word and help you plant these life-changing truths in your heart. Otherwise, you risk becoming a Christian who knows a lot of things but struggles in the areas where victory is most needed. Head knowledge alone cannot produce the power needed for change, though it's valuable to have a solid knowledge base. What we're after is depth—the kind that touches the core of who you are and aligns you with God's power.

A little about my own background—I was raised in a very strict denominational church. We walked in the light we had, and that's important. However, like many denominations, we believed we were the guardians of the "real" truth. Many of us grew up thinking, "We have all the truth." But the closer you get to God, the more you realize that true wisdom allows you to respect and learn from others in the body of Christ. Wisdom is being like Joseph, with a coat of many colors, enriched by the revelations from different streams of the faith. We don't have to be limited to just one expression of God's truth.

In my upbringing, we were very focused on staying within the Word—and while that's a good thing, often, it became limiting. For instance, some people in the church said, "If musical instruments aren't mentioned in the New Testament, we won't use them." And so, we sang a cappella. There were no drums, no pianos, no organs. While we were devoted to following the Word, we often missed the broader illumination it offers. It's important to follow the Word, yes, but also to understand that God's light shines beyond our limited interpretations.

And here's the beauty of it: while we now walk in the New Covenant, which is a better covenant, we can still draw life and wisdom from the Old Testament. There are treasures there that speak to us today. God's Word is timeless, and the principles found in the Torah and the Psalms, for example, continue to speak life and truth to us in ways that can enrich our walk with Christ.

When I was growing up in church, we placed a significant emphasis on Scripture memorization. Let me give you an example that highlights just how deeply ingrained this practice was. One Sunday, I watched a preacher from my denomination stand before the congregation and say, "Today, I'm not going to preach. Instead, I'm going to quote the entire book of 1 Corinthians." And that's exactly what he did—without notes or even a Bible in hand. He stood there and flawlessly recited the entire letter, from chapter one, verse one, all the way through. It took him about 50 minutes, the same amount of time it would take someone to sit and read it. Not a single fumble or error, just pure memorization. We, in the pews, followed along with our Bibles open, marveling at the precision of his memory.

But here's the thing, and this is crucial: It's not about how much Scripture you know. It's not even about being able to quote large portions of the Bible. The real power lies in being able to drill down, to dig deep and extract the nuggets, the gems, and the gold from the Word, and getting them into your heart.

That preacher, as brilliant as he was—he had a PhD, he knew Greek and Hebrew, and possessed an amazing memory—still had limitations. After the service, I could have approached him and said, "Pastor, you quoted 1 Corinthians 12, where Paul talks about the gifts of the Holy Spirit. Do you believe those gifts, like prophecy and working miracles, are for us today?" His response, undoubtedly, would have been, "Oh, no! That all ended with the first-century apostles." Or, if I asked about 1 Corinthians 14, where Paul gives instructions on the use of tongues in church services and personal prayer, his answer would likely have been the same, "Oh, no, that's not for us today. That ceased when the last apostle died."

He was a good preacher, but he had no revelatory knowledge of the present-day miracle-working power of God.

You see, you can know vast portions of Scripture, but without understanding, without revelation, it doesn't transform your life. It's the light of God's Word, the understanding you gain from it, that brings victory. Simply having head knowledge doesn't move mountains; it's the deep, heart-rooted truths that make a difference. The Bible is indeed a remarkable book—filled with stories that captivate and inspire, from Joseph, who was sold into slavery by his brothers and rose to prominence in Egypt (a clear type of Christ), to David's triumphs, and ultimately to Jesus, our Messiah. The Bible is packed with real-life drama that no human could ever invent. It's a book like no other.

But to truly benefit from it, you have to go beyond merely knowing the stories. You need to meditate on the Word until it becomes alive in you, until it moves from head knowledge to heart revelation. That's where the power is, and that's what produces victory in your life.

If you don't make that transition from intellect to heart, then when you face life's challenges, all the knowledge in the world won't help you. You could be quoting scriptures left and right, but without true belief in the heart, it won't work. Life will present you with battles that are too complex for mere knowledge to resolve, and you can't just shoot random scriptures at the problem and expect it to disappear. You need the living Word deeply rooted in your heart.

So, let me ask you: When do you prepare for battle? Do you start getting your weapons ready on the front line when the enemy is already shooting at you? Of course not! Preparation begins long before the battle starts. Soldiers train, weapons are developed, and strategies are tested long before the first shot is fired. The same principle applies spiritually. You don't wait until the heat of battle to begin preparing your heart.

Unfortunately, many Christians do exactly that. When they're suddenly hit with a crisis—be it sickness, financial trouble, or a spiritual attack—they start frantically quoting scriptures, often with little understanding or conviction behind the words. They heard the preacher say, "By His stripes, I'm healed," or "Speak the Word, and it will work," but it's all coming from the head, not from a heart full of faith. And when it doesn't work, they're left confused, wondering why the Word isn't producing the results they expected.

The truth is, if you wait until you're in the middle of a crisis to start building up your faith, you're already behind. Just like soldiers prepare for war months or even years in advance, we must continually be filling our hearts with the Word so that when the time comes, we're ready. When the pressure is on, what's in your heart is what will come out of your mouth. If your heart is full of faith, grounded in God's Word, then when you speak, creative power is released, and the enemy must flee. But if all you have is intellectual knowledge, it won't move a spiritual enemy.

Jesus made this clear: *"Out of the abundance of the heart, the mouth speaks"* (Matthew 12:34). It's not enough for the Word to simply be present in your heart—it must abound in your heart. Whatever is flooding your heart is what will come out when the pressure is on. If your heart is filled with the Word, you'll speak life, power, and victory. But if your heart is filled with distractions, doubt, or mere head knowledge, that's what will come out in the heat of battle.

This is why it's so important to labor in the Word, to meditate on it day and night so that your heart is full of God's promises. When your heart is full, your mouth will speak, and what you say will carry the creative power of God. *"Then God said, 'Let there be light,' and there was light"* (Genesis 1:3). God spoke before the light appeared. The creative power flowed from His words, and that's exactly how it works for us. We must speak in faith before we see the manifestation.

And here's a powerful truth: What you are unwilling or unable to loudly and publicly proclaim will never manifest in your life. If you truly believe God's Word, you won't hesitate to speak it out boldly. Many people backpedal when it comes time to declare their faith publicly. Why? Because they aren't fully convinced. But when the Word is alive in you—when you have those gold nuggets of truth deeply rooted in your heart—you'll speak with boldness and confidence, no matter what.

I know this to be true from personal experience. I have been in situations where I was completely convinced of God's Word and saw it work powerfully in my life. I won't apologize for what the Word says, and I won't back down. I know the power of speaking God's truth, and I also know the devastation that comes from living without that revelation. When I began to speak God's Word over my life and believe it fully in my heart, everything began to change for the better. Now, instead of facing defeat, I minister the Gospel around the world, sharing the full counsel of God, which includes His provision, His healing, and His power.

I am fully convinced that God's Word works. The convictions I hold today didn't come from mere head knowledge or from what other preachers said—they came from laboring in the Word until it became part of me. That is the pathway to victory: when the Word is no longer just something you know intellectually, but something you live and breathe.

Can you imagine the day when we all stand before God, and many believers will realize that while they loved Jesus, they never fully walked in the light of His Word? They'll see the truth in Heaven, but we have the opportunity to walk in it now. Don't wait for eternity to experience the fullness of God's promises—begin to fill your heart with His Word today, and watch as it transforms your life.

When Abraham was preparing to make that critical sacrifice, splitting the animals in half as part of the covenant, vultures descended, trying to devour the offering. Abraham had to fight off these birds, and in many ways, this represents the spiritual battle we all face. The enemy constantly tries to steal the revelations and blessings God has for us, just as those vultures tried to take Abraham's offering. In the same way, we must be vigilant in fighting off evil spirits, false teachings, and lies that try to consume what God is doing in our lives.

Abraham didn't let those vultures come near his sacrifice. Similarly, we must stand firm and say, "No, devil! You won't steal what God is birthing in my life!" Sometimes, the enemy comes in strong, like those vultures we see today—big, intimidating, and persistent—but we have to fight back and refuse to let them take what belongs to us. Hallelujah! Thank you, Jesus. We must fight for what is ours and walk in the light of God's Word.

What comes out of your mouth will determine the course of your life. Until you can boldly declare God's promises, you won't fully possess them. Now is the time to rise up and be bold in your faith, letting it shine through your words and confessions. Praise the Lord! This is a mystery of faith—this element of speaking and holding firmly to God's living truth. We may not fully understand how it works, but this is how God designed His Kingdom to operate. Remember when God said, *"Let there be light,"* and there was light? That's how the system works: through faith-filled words. This is God's world, His universe, and these are the laws He has set in motion. It's up to us to discover them, align with them, and work with them for our lives to prosper.

Let's take a look at one of the most powerful verses in the Bible. Jesus said:

> "For assuredly, I say to you, whoever says to this mountain, 'Be removed and be cast into the sea,' and does not doubt in his heart, but believes that those things he says will be done, he will have whatever he says."
>
> — Mark 11:23

Praise the Lord! This is the importance of filling your heart with the hidden manna, the revelatory truths God is revealing to you. When your heart is full of God's Word and His direction for your life, you're able to speak with power and authority. It's like loading a cannon—when your heart is filled with the Word, you can unleash it with explosive results!

But remember, the cannon must be loaded first. You can't speak from an empty heart. Your words flow from the abundance of your heart, and when it's full of God's truth, you will speak with boldness, and situations will change. That's how you can speak to a sinful habit or to financial lack and declare in the name of Jesus, "You will no longer have control over me!" You need to speak it out loud so that even the devil hears it, letting him know you're done with compromise. Too often, people struggle because they aren't willing to make that bold declaration. But when you say it—when you declare your victory over sin or debt or sickness—you're stepping into the authority Christ has given you. You're telling the enemy, "I'm done with you!"

We see this principle in other areas of life too. You can speak to financial debt and declare, "In the name of Jesus, you are paid off and uprooted from my life!" But you need to be filled with the Word for your words to have power. Too often, people are quoting scriptures without seeing results because they're just repeating what they've heard others say. There's no personal conviction behind it. You need to get into the Word for yourself, meditate on it, and let it fill your heart. Only then can you speak with the kind of authority that moves mountains.

Don't just grab any scripture—seek God for a specific Word to stand on. Find your Word from God. It has to be alive in you, not borrowed from someone else's journey. When David faced Goliath, he didn't let someone else pick his stones. He went down to the brook and chose five smooth stones for himself. He was preparing for his own fight. He knew Goliath had four brothers, and he wasn't taking any chances. In the same way, you must find the scriptures that work for you. Labor in the Word, find those precious gems, and let them settle into your heart. When you're full of the Word, you can speak with authority and watch as mountains move in your life.

Jesus said that whoever says to this mountain, *"Be removed," and does not doubt, will have whatever they say.* That means if you're not talking to your mountains—whether they be sin, sickness, debt, or fear—they won't move! You must speak to them, but you can't do that from an empty heart. Your heart has to be full of faith and truth, filled with God's promises. When you speak from that place of fullness, mountains will be cast into the sea.

> Death and life are in the power of the tongue,
> And those who love it will eat its fruit.
>
> — Proverbs 18:21

How much life you enjoy depends on how much you're speaking. When you speak death, it comes. When you talk failure and defeat, they manifest. I've seen people speak negativity into their lives, and when those things come to pass, they wonder why. It's not a miracle—it's a law. Whether or not you understand it, spiritual laws are at work.

I've had to lovingly correct people before when they were speaking negatively over their lives, telling them to choose their words carefully. You can choose to speak life, and when you do, it flows. God commands us to choose life, but we have to speak it. It's not enough to know the Word in your head—you have to let it fill your heart and flow from your mouth.

The Holy Spirit is moving right now, and some of you reading this are beginning to recognize that the words you've been speaking have been steering you off course. Words of hopelessness and unbelief have shaped your path, but that can change right now. You have the power to set a new course for your life by choosing to speak words of faith. Declare, "From this day forward, I'm going in the right direction. I'm free from sin, sickness, and disease in the name of Jesus!"

Many have told me, "Pastor Steven, it's just a matter of time before you get sick, like the rest of us." And I've had to correct them, saying, "No, I won't." When your heart is full of God's healing Word, you don't beg for healing—you command sickness to leave. God isn't moved by tears or pleading. He responds to faith-filled declarations of His Word. When you're full of the Word, you'll no longer say, "Oh God, heal me." Instead, you'll say, "This sickness cannot stay in my body any longer. In the name of Jesus, it's got to go!"

The devil will bow to the name of Jesus, but only when your heart is full of faith. If you're just flinging scriptures out of your head without the power of conviction, it won't work. It's not enough to rattle off verses—you need to have the Word rooted in your heart.

We are living in perilous times, as Jesus said. But no matter how difficult the days may be, you can stand strong by staying filled with the Word of God. When your heart is full, your mouth will speak, and you'll walk in victory. Hallelujah! God's Word is powerful, and when you declare it from a heart of faith, the enemy has no choice but to flee.

Prophecies and promises from God often come with conditions, requiring us to do our part to see them fulfilled. Many people don't realize that most prophecies are conditional. It's not enough to just receive a word from the Lord; we have to take action. If we fulfill our part, we commit God to do His. And we know that God always does His part—He is ever faithful. But if we don't, those prophecies can become like unfulfilled promises, sitting there without producing any results.

Without our participation, these prophetic words turn into something like horoscopes—just vague declarations: "This week is prosperity week," or "Next week is blessing week." Months and even years pass by, and people wonder why nothing changes. It's not because the prophecy was false. Often, the words themselves are accurate; they could very well be in alignment with what God wants to do. The issue is that without our active engagement—without God's Word taking root in our hearts—there's no supernatural manifestation of those blessings in our lives.

This reminds me of what happens in the church today. Many believers have a "machine-gun mentality" with Scripture—they just fire off all these verses without focusing or being anchored in any particular one. They'll declare, "By His stripes, I'm healed," or "I'm blessed," without truly standing on specific, revelatory words that speak to their situation. And then they wonder why it doesn't work. It's because, like shade-tree mechanics trying to fix a modern car without the proper tools, they lack the depth, understanding, and focus needed to make their declarations effective.

Let me explain. If you want your car fixed today, you don't take it to someone who only knows how to change the oil or fix the brakes. Modern cars are so advanced that you need specialized scanners, tools, and knowledge specific to each make and model. The same is true spiritually. There are too many in the church who know just enough to speak the right lingo and go through the motions, but they aren't operating with the full power of God's Word because their hearts are cluttered with distractions, doubts, or shallow understanding.

In closing, I want to share something that happened to Neville Johnson, an apostle friend of mine from Australia. He was a deeply spiritual man who prayed a lot, but one day, he learned a hard lesson about the power of words. He told me that while he was in his house, a door to the spirit realm opened up. Perceiving it, he jokingly said, "Come on in!" Without realizing it, he had just given permission for an unknown entity to enter his space. Suddenly, a massive demonic creature came through that door into his house. He immediately tried to cast it out, but the demon responded, "Too late—you told me I could come."

He explained to me that it took him two weeks to get that demon out of his life. Every time he tried to command it to leave, the demon would say, "You told me I could come in." He couldn't say, "I was just joking," because in the spiritual realm, your words have power, whether you're serious or not. Praise the Lord. This experience taught him—and should teach us all—the importance of being very careful with what we say.

Jesus said we would be *judged by the words we speak* (Matthew 12:36). That doesn't mean we can't have fun or enjoy life—the joy of the Lord is our strength—but we must be mindful of what comes out of our mouths. Often, when people aren't filled with the Word, they resort to careless speech, joking, or making crude remarks. God warns us in Ephesians 5:4 not to let coarse jesting come out of our mouths. This kind of talk is an indicator that something is wrong in the heart.

The spirit realm is real, and it's not something to take lightly. Whenever I've been in the spirit realm, I've only spoken what God wanted me to say, or I've stayed silent. In the second Heaven, where Satan has his strongholds, it is particularly dangerous because of the spiritual warfare taking place. You either speak what God directs, or you remain quiet. These are things we must learn as we grow spiritually.

Let me give you an example from my past. About 50 years ago, I was sitting in the back seat of the car with my brothers as my father drove us into a small town. As we slowed down, my father—who knew a lot of Scripture but didn't fully understand the power of words—said, "I'll tell you one thing: if anyone's going to get a ticket in this town, it'll be me. You watch, it'll be me."

Within seconds, we saw police lights flashing behind us. The officer pulled us over, and sure enough, my dad got a speeding ticket. My dad's response? "Well, that just beats anything I've ever seen!" He couldn't understand how he had basically spoken his own ticket into existence. My father never grasped the principle of speaking life or death with our words, but that's exactly what he had done—he got what he said. He lived his whole life never fully understanding the power of Proverbs 18:21, *"Death and life are in the power of the tongue."*

It's not just about avoiding profanity or negative language; you must be careful not to speak death into your own life by constantly confessing negativity. You could be in the camp of believers, but like the spies who brought back a negative report from the Promised Land, your words could be full of doubt and fear, and that can crush the faith of an entire assembly. On the other hand, you could be like Joshua and Caleb, who confidently declared, *"We can take this land!"* God had already promised it to them—they just needed to speak in alignment with His Word.

It's your choice today: will you speak life or death? Your words are powerful, and when you speak in faith, based on God's promises, mountains will move, and your life will change. So, speak life over your situation, and trust that God's Word will never fail.

Chapter Twenty-One

Faith and Frankincense: The Aroma That Pleases God

Let's dive into Leviticus 24, starting from verse 5, where we encounter the table of showbread. This table wasn't just an ordinary piece of furniture; it was a heavenly blueprint, a commandment from God revealed to Moses. In turn, Moses entrusted the creation of this sacred object to Bezalel, a master artisan. Bezalel wasn't just skilled; he was divinely gifted in working with gold, precious metals, gemstones, and fine cloth. His craftsmanship was integral in constructing the table of showbread, an object far more complex than it might initially seem.

The showbread, which rested on the table, held a remarkable quality—it remained fresh for seven days, never growing stale or moldy, even without preservatives. This was because it was perpetually in the presence of the Lord, who dwelt between the cherubim on the Ark of the Covenant. Each of the 12 loaves, representing the 12 tribes of Israel, weighed a significant 11 pounds.

Scripture outlines the preparation and placement of the showbread:

> "And you shall take fine flour and bake twelve cakes with it. Two-tenths of an ephah shall be in each cake. You shall set them in two rows, six in a row, on the pure gold table before the Lord. And you shall put pure frankincense on each row, that it may be on the bread for a memorial, an offering made by fire to the Lord. Every Sabbath he shall set it in order before the Lord continually, being taken from the children of Israel by an everlasting covenant. And it shall be for Aaron and his sons, and they shall eat it in a holy place; for it is most holy to him from the offerings of the Lord made by fire, by a perpetual statute."
>
> — Leviticus 24:5-9

This bread, also known as the "bread of the presence," is deeply symbolic. Theologians often describe the showbread as a "type" or symbol in the Old Testament that points to a greater truth in the New Testament. In this case, the showbread represents the Word of God, which, like bread, must remain fresh and sustaining in our lives.

The bread was replaced every Sabbath with newly baked loaves, but the old loaves were still fresh and moist, a powerful reminder that God's Word is always alive and relevant, no matter how many centuries have passed. The outgoing and incoming priests would consume the old showbread in a holy place, signifying their participation in God's provision and presence.

The command to place pure frankincense on the bread is particularly intriguing. Frankincense, from its earliest mentions in Scripture, is a symbol of faith. The presence of frankincense on the showbread signifies that faith must accompany the Word of God. As this passage reminds us, the Word must be mixed with faith to be effective: *"For indeed the gospel was preached to us as well as to them; but the word which they heard did not profit them, not being mixed with faith in those who heard it"* (Hebrews 4:2).

Just as the bread was always fresh, our faith must be living and active, continually renewed by the Word of God. Frankincense was one of the gifts presented to Jesus by the wise men, and at that time, it was more valuable than gold. This reflects the spiritual truth found in 1 Peter 1:7, where faith is described as being more precious than gold, a faith that is tested and refined through trials.

In essence, the showbread, with frankincense sprinkled on it, teaches us that receiving God's best for our lives comes from a combination of hearing the Word and receiving it in faith. Without faith, even the Word of God will not profit us. And just as the showbread remained fresh, our faith must continually be sustained by a fresh and living Word.

Now, when there is a supernatural manifestation of the Holy Spirit, what does it mean when you begin to smell frankincense in the spirit realm? Number one, it means that God is giving you His very best. Number two, frankincense represents faith. You must receive God's best by faith, understanding that the actual manifestation of what you're believing for will come to fruition.

Prophet Kenneth E. Hagin once shared a powerful experience in his book *I Believe in Visions*. He explained how, after delivering a message one night, the congregation was drawn into a deep spirit of prayer. As they prayed around the altar, Hagin felt prompted to sit on the platform steps, where he began singing in tongues as the Holy Spirit led him.

In that moment, Hagin saw Jesus standing before him. Jesus told him that He had come to answer Hagin's prayer—a prayer concerning his wife, Oretha, who had been suffering from a goiter that was causing serious health concerns. Hagin had sensed for years that Oretha might pass away at a young age, and with her condition worsening, he was concerned the time had come.

Hagin had previously poured out his heart to God, reminding Him of the sacrifices both he and his wife had made for the ministry. He asked the Lord to allow him to keep his wife. Jesus responded by telling him that Oretha should undergo surgery and assured him that she would live, not die. Although Hagin had felt for a long time that surgery would be fatal for his wife, Jesus gave him peace, saying that, without divine intervention, Oretha would indeed die—but He had heard Hagin's prayers and had come to intervene.

What touched Hagin the most was when Jesus told him that He was answering the prayer simply because Hagin had asked in faith. He expressed how He longs to do more for His children if they would only trust Him and believe His Word rather than approach Him in doubt or unbelief.

With this reassurance from the Lord, Hagin and Oretha faced the situation with joy, knowing that she would survive the surgery. Despite the doctors' concerns, they had confidence because God had already revealed the outcome.

This vision and encounter deeply impacted Hagin, leaving him with a powerful reminder of the goodness of God and the importance of asking in faith.

When we combine our faith with God's promises, it allows us to receive deeply sacred things from the Lord. Here's what I want you to do: Write down three things you want God to do for you personally.

Take some time to write out three personal desires or needs that you want God to fulfill. These are things that you can actively believe Him for. Take the Word, the Bread of Life, and sprinkle it with your faith—your frankincense. Mix it together, and you'll receive what you desire to have. He wants you to receive these blessings. He longs for you to have them, but He cannot act if you are in fear, because He cannot violate His Word. You must be in faith. Praise God!

After you've written them down, find small pictures representing each of these desires. Place these pictures on your refrigerator door or in another spot that you frequently see—like your bathroom mirror where you get ready each morning. Let these visual reminders be a constant encouragement. Every time you see them, say, "Jesus, I'm mixing my faith, my frankincense, with Your Word. You are going to fulfill this for me. Jesus, You've got this. You will make it happen."

When you say this, speak with faith and understanding, knowing that He wants to do this for you. He longs to fulfill these desires. And He will. As you hold firm in faith, trust Him, and stay steadfast in His Word, He will bring it to pass.

Remember, it's not just about having the bread of His Word alone—it must be mixed with the right ingredients. Your faith, your frankincense, must be sprinkled on that Word. Praise God!

Chapter Twenty-Two

Faithful Restraint: Trusting Without Overreaching

In the Book of Proverbs we come across a prayer that says, *"Feed me with the food allotted to me"* (Proverbs 30:8). This is a heartfelt, prayerful request to God, asking for the specific provision He has ordained for us. The New American Standard Bible says, *"Feed me with the food that is my portion,"* emphasizing that God has a unique portion, specifically tailored for each of His people. It's not just about physical nourishment—it's about what God has prepared for us, spiritually and in life, that is perfectly designed for our journey.

Let's explore this in the context of God's provision being like a meal. God has a *meal plan* for each of us, and just like at a family dinner, every part of the meal is important. Imagine sitting around a dinner table with young children. The mom is serving dinner, and she doles out different portions of food: maybe some salad, some mashed potatoes, a piece of chicken, and perhaps dessert to finish off the meal. Now, if the children had their way, they might only want to eat the mac and cheese or jump straight to dessert. They might resist the vegetables or the healthier options, just wanting what tastes good in the moment.

But the mom knows what's best for her children. She makes sure they get a balanced meal because she understands that they need more than just the sweet or easy parts—they need the nutrients from the vegetables, the proteins from the chicken, and the balance that will help them grow strong. Spiritually, we are often like those children. We want the blessings, the comfort, the "desserts" of life, but we might resist the more challenging parts—the "vegetables" that God knows we need to grow and mature in faith.

I remember when I was a child, growing up on a farm, we ate what we grew, and I loved some of the crops like peanuts, strawberries, and corn. But there were other foods I absolutely resisted, like collard greens and Brussels sprouts. The Brussels sprouts especially triggered a gag reflex for me—I later learned that there's actually an enzyme in certain people that causes this reaction! Back then, though, my parents didn't care about enzymes. You ate what was on your plate. And despite my resistance, those foods were good for me.

In the same way, we often push back against the portions God gives us in life. We might not like certain experiences, trials, or lessons that He knows are necessary for our growth. But just like my parents insisted I eat my vegetables because they knew what was best for me, God knows what is best for us, even if we don't understand or like it in the moment.

When we pray, *"Feed me with the food allotted to me,"* it's a brave prayer. We're not just asking God for the blessings or the easy things. We're asking Him for what He knows we need, even if that includes challenges, growth opportunities, or lessons we'd rather avoid. It's a surrender to His wisdom and a true walk of faith.

We're all in different cycles of spiritual growth. So, what God, in His infinite wisdom, does is He sees the various needs that we all have in these different stages, and the *food* is actually served differently for each person. Now, I'm in my late 50s. I don't get excited about applesauce anymore. But when I was a little child, I remember eating applesauce out of a cup—and I liked it. These days, applesauce doesn't really do much for me.

What does that mean? It means that as we go through life, as we grow and mature, things change. Even as children, our teeth develop, our digestive systems mature, and eventually, we get older and find out about new flavors like peppers, spicy food, and so on. So, we're all in different phases, different stages.

What we need to do is be patient and accept the portion God is serving us during the season of our lives, even if we might think, "Lord, this isn't the meal I was hoping for." Or we may say, "Lord, I'd rather be in a different moment today. Can't we go to a different restaurant?" But when God says, "This is where you're at, and this is what you need right now," we have to trust Him, receive it, and walk in it, even if it's a bit perplexing.

Why? Because not everyone participates in God's food program—allowing themselves to be fed by Him. Some Christians love God and are on their way to Heaven, but they're going to eat what they want. No one, not even the Holy Spirit, can tell them otherwise.

And that's their choice—God honors our free will. But when you yield yourself to the Lord, using your free will to say, "God, I trust

You," He leads you down some very interesting paths—paths designed to mold you into the image of Christ.

Now, let's go further with this concept.

> "You have skirted this mountain long enough; turn northward."
>
> — Deuteronomy 2:3

He's commanding the people to stop circling the mountain and move forward.

> "You are about to pass through the territory of your brethren, the descendants of Esau, who live in Seir; and they will be afraid of you. Therefore watch yourselves carefully. Do not meddle with them, for I will not give you any of their land, no, not so much as one footstep, because I have given Mount Seir to Esau as a possession."
>
> — Deuteronomy 2:4-5

In other words, God tells Moses to warn the people that they're about to pass by land that looks desirable. They might think, "Wow, this is where I want to settle! This is perfect for me and my family." But God says, "No." He won't give them even one square foot of it. Not an inch.

> "When we passed beyond our brethren, the descendants of Esau who dwell in Seir, away from the road of the plain, away from Elath and Ezion Geber, we turned and passed

> by way of the Wilderness of Moab. Then the Lord said to me, 'Do not harass Moab, nor contend with them in battle, for I will not give you any of their land as a possession, because I have given Ar to the descendants of Lot.'"
>
> — Deuteronomy 2:8-9

What I want to share with you today is how to balance the promises in the Word of God with the reality of what your portion is. There are over 10,000 promises in the Bible, and I've heard people say—and even sing—that all of them are ours. But here's the reality: All the promises of God are yes and amen, but they aren't all for you. Even if you lived as long as Methuselah—969 years—you wouldn't be able to personally manifest over 10,000 promises.

So, what we need to do is think through the Word of God carefully, lest we fall into the trap of assuming everything is ours, when in reality, God may be saying, "That's not what I'm feeding you with." Others may be eating that, and it may be exactly what they need. It might be their spiritual T-bone steak or filet mignon, but that doesn't mean it's meant for you. God has something different, something specific, tailored for you.

You have to be careful not to look at what others are receiving and desire it for yourself. God knows what's best for you, and He knows exactly what you need. So, rather than comparing portions, we should trust that what He is serving us is exactly what we need for our growth.

> "The Lord spoke to me, saying: 'This day you are to cross over at Ar, the boundary of Moab. And when you come near the people of Ammon, do not harass them or

> meddle with them, for I will not give you any of the land of the people of Ammon as a possession, because I have given it to the descendants of Lot.'"
>
> — Deuteronomy 2:17-19

Doesn't this sound repetitive? God is making it clear—certain lands, certain blessings, are not for the Israelites. They're reserved for someone else. But don't worry, God hasn't forgotten about you.

"Rise, take your journey, and cross over the River Arnon. Look, I have given into your hand Sihon the Amorite, king of Heshbon, and his land. Begin to possess it, and engage him in battle."

Here, God reveals their portion. This land is theirs, but they still have to go in and fight for it.

Verse 36 provides a summation of what happens when you pursue what is truly your portion: *"There was not one city too strong for us. The Lord our God delivered all to us."* You see, you can have it all, but it has to be the *all* that pertains to you.

Some people want everything, but we each have a portion. Knowing your portion and staying in your lane is essential. It keeps you from burnout and ensures you're walking in the fullness of what God has called you to.

You can't do everything. I know my calling isn't to have the largest church in the world, especially in a rural area. Dr. Paul Yonggi Cho, on the other hand, was called to grow his church to 800,000 members. He knew this when his church only had 20 members—he had a clear sense of his portion from God.

Meanwhile, God told me to focus on daily television ministry, which allows me to reach a satellite footprint of over two billion people. That's my portion, and I'm walking in it, just as Dr. Cho walked in his.

There are a lot of believers trying to step onto someone else's property, like Lot's land, saying, "I can do it too," or "I belong here," when God is saying, "That's not what I'm trying to feed you."

They're like little children saying, "But I don't want to eat what You want me to, Lord. I want what they're eating!" And the Lord responds, "They're not after depth, they're not after being conformed into the image of My Son." But the child says, "I don't care—I want what they have."

You have to find your place. You have to know your identity, know your purpose, and know what God is serving you on your plate. Praise God!

If you want to claim something from God's Word as your portion, you can find it in there somewhere. You might say, "Pastor Steven, I'm not sure if it's God's will for me or not, but I want something over here, so I'm going to find a scripture for it." And I guarantee you, you can cook something up. People have been doing that for centuries—they pull it, they grab it, and say, "God promised it!"

Yes, God promised it, but not to you. Some don't care—they take it anyway and try to manipulate God's Word to make it say what they want it to say. So you must be careful not to do that. Stay in your lane, or you'll end up frustrated, unhappy, and even spiritually barren. You might lose your spiritual awareness because you're eating something that's not meant for you. You're dry on the inside because you're consuming what wasn't designed for you.

God has the right to test us. He never tempts us, but He does test us to prove us, grow us, and build our character. The devil, on the other hand, does tempt us with the intent to destroy us. Now, let's look at the temptation Jesus faced and learn how important it is to know what your portion is—and what is not.

Let's go to Matthew chapter 3. I'm so glad you're reading along, hungry for the things of God and wanting to know Him more. I get uncomfortable around Christians who think they know everything about God, like they're God Junior. These are the folks who can't go deep—they can talk wide on general topics, but if you try to go deep, they're uninterested. What can you discuss with them? Not much, just stick to the weather or other light topics.

> When He had been baptized, Jesus came up immediately from the water; and behold, the heavens were opened to Him, and He saw the Spirit of God descending like a dove and alighting upon Him. And suddenly a voice came from heaven, saying, "This is My beloved Son, in whom I am well pleased."
>
> — Matthew 3:16-17

This is key. The Father never said that about Adam—He said it about Jesus, the second Adam. The first Adam did okay for a while, but when the tempter came and started reasoning with him, he fell. You can't reason with the devil! We're here for 80, maybe 90 years—if by strength, some may live to 100—but the devil has been here for thousands of years. He knows how to twist reasoning. You can't engage him on that level. You need absolutes—yes or no. There's no middle ground.

Now, after the Father affirms Jesus as His beloved Son, we move into chapter 4, verse 1, where it says: *"Then Jesus was led up by the Spirit into the wilderness to be tempted by the devil."* The leading of the Holy Spirit is imperative, especially in major events. You must have that inward witness of the Spirit.

After fasting for 40 days and nights, Jesus was profoundly hungry—extremely so. At this stage, the body has exhausted its fat reserves, and if nourishment isn't restored, it will begin breaking down muscle and even vital organs in a desperate effort to survive. This is when true hunger sets in, signaling a critical window that cannot be ignored.

This is when the devil comes in, intentionally targeting the point of maximum weakness, and says in verse 3, *"If You are the Son of God, command that these stones become bread."* The devil tries to cast doubt on Jesus' identity and tempts Him to satisfy His hunger in a way that's outside of His God-given portion.

But Jesus refuses to take the bait. His hunger wasn't the issue—the issue was the devil trying to make Him step outside of what was allowed by God. Just as God told the Israelites not to touch certain lands, the devil was tempting Jesus to meet His needs in an illegitimate way. And turning stones into bread wasn't on the Father's menu for Jesus. Neither is it on ours.

You see, the devil feeds people in ways that God never would. Even some Christians fall for this—they'll justify stepping outside their portion, saying, "Well, I had to do it." But when you walk with God, you must be willing to stay hungry until God feeds you the right way.

I'm familiar with a very godly prophet who has since graduated to Heaven. When he was young in ministry, he found himself facing tremendous personal financial need. Newly in full-time ministry, with a wife to care for, he was in a situation where he thought, "I can call so-and-so, and they'll help me out." But God spoke to him and said, "You touch that phone, I'm through with you—through with trying to develop you in the school of the Spirit."

You see, we all know how to turn stones into bread—not in the sense of performing miracles, but we know how to work systems. We know how to pull levers, make calls, and manipulate situations to make things happen. But when you play games like that, God will pull back, and you won't enter the deeper school of the Spirit He's trying to lead you into—the one I'm sharing with you here.

This is the advanced school of the Spirit. And though it's a challenging journey, there is outrageous joy in it—outrageous manifestations of the glory and power of God and divine provision that only He can bring.

And as the temptations continued, did you notice that Jesus remained hungry? He didn't get a snack break. No angel slipped Him a Snickers bar. The test persisted, and He still didn't eat. This teaches us a thought-provoking lesson: sometimes, you have to stay hungry and wait for God's provision. It's in that waiting where true character is formed.

Let's move to the next temptation:

> Then the devil took Him up into the holy city, set Him on the pinnacle of the temple.
>
> — Matthew 4:5

How many Christians have jumped off the pinnacle? I can't tell you how many come to me, broken and battered, because they took a leap based on temptation rather than God's Word.

The devil tries to push Jesus again, saying, *"If You are the Son of God, throw Yourself down, for it is written..."* The devil can quote Scripture—and in this case, he even quotes it in context, a messianic word about the Father's protection over Jesus. But even though it was true, it wasn't Jesus' portion to jump.

This is a dangerous area. Some Christians say, "I found a promise from God, and I'm going to claim it!" But the question is—is it truly yours? If it's not, you could be the one sending an email to me, broken and disappointed, because you took a leap you weren't supposed to take.

The devil is slick. He's very cunning. You'll never beat him in the flesh, and you'll never outsmart him because he's been around for thousands of years. He's not impressed by a high IQ—actually, that makes him laugh because people with high IQs usually lean on it, and he thinks, "Oh, this'll be easy."

What the devil was doing with Jesus was similar. He said, "Look, all the rabbis have taught for centuries that when the Messiah shows up—and You're claiming to be Him—the Messiah will do a sign. This is Your moment! Jump. Let them all see You jump, and as You fall, the angels will catch You. That will be the sign." They would all say, "That's it! This is the One!"

That expectation was deeply rooted in Jewish culture. The devil was playing on it. "Look, You've even got a Bible verse! What else do You need? Jump!"

But Jesus didn't do it.

Every nation carries its own defining characteristic, something that shapes its culture and values. The Jews crave a sign. The Greeks are captivated by wisdom. And Americans? We are the entertainment capital of the universe. Endless sports, movies, and shows—a never-ending supply of distraction and decadence.

But here's the reality: The promises of God won't work in the wrong setting. I didn't say they weren't true. All the promises of God are yes and amen, including Psalm 91:10-12. But if that promise isn't part of God's plan for you at this time, don't jump. If you do, you're putting God to the test, and Scripture forbids that.

"Well, Pastor Steven, if you had faith, you'd jump!" That's just trying to shame people. Now you've pressured them, and they think, "Well, I guess I should jump." So they jump—not because God said to, but because they were shamed into it. And now, they've dug themselves a deeper hole they'll eventually have to climb out of.

But Jesus said: *"It is written again: You shall not put the Lord your God to the test"* (Matthew 4:7 NASB). In Greek, it's implied that when you do, you're provoking God.

Now, a pattern is forming as we move into the final temptation.

> Again, the devil took Him up on an exceedingly high mountain, and showed Him all the kingdoms of the world and their glory. And he said to Him, "All these things I will give You if You will fall down and worship me."
>
> — Matthew 4:8-9

Notice Satan didn't ask Jesus to serve him—because who you worship is who you'll serve. If Satan could get Jesus to worship him, the rest would follow. Satan was after worship, the very thing that got him kicked out of heaven. He hasn't changed; he still wants to be worshiped today.

"Away with you, Satan! For it is written, 'You shall worship the Lord your God, and Him only you shall serve.'"

This time, Jesus rebuked the devil. He didn't just resist like before—He said, *"Away with you, Satan!"* He didn't do that the first two times. Here's why: Every time you resist the devil, you get stronger. The more you resist, the stronger you get.

He resisted the first temptation, and He got stronger. He resisted the second, and He got stronger. By the third, He was so strong that He not only resisted—He rebuked the devil outright. Resist the devil, and he will flee.

Then the devil left Him, and behold, angels came and ministered to Him.

Now it's time to eat. Jesus didn't take shortcuts or turn stones into bread. He waited, and now God provided. Not just any meal—a meal served by angels.

"Well, Pastor Steven, what do you expect me to do—starve?" My answer: Hang in there. I know you're hungry. I know you have needs. But aren't you glad Jesus didn't eat out of bounds? He waited for God to feed Him. That's why the Father said, *"This is My beloved Son, in whom I am well pleased."* Adam blew it, but this One got it right.

The devil walked away, confused. "What did I just run into?" He ran into the second Adam.

Some theologians claim Jesus couldn't have sinned. If that were true, the whole thing would be a farce. Of course, He could have sinned. He laid down His deity and walked as a sinless man, just like Adam. He could've messed up, but He didn't. He stood firm on the Word of God, and He stood on the Word that was His portion. He didn't grab a promise that wasn't meant for Him, unlike how many Christians today grab scriptures out of context and later on wonder why they don't work.

It's like looking at Lot's inheritance and saying, "I want that!" But God says, "No, that's not your portion." Yet some pursue it anyway. As a result, they end up frustrated, unhappy, living under tension, and ultimately outside of God's perfect will for their lives.

When you're in the center of God's will, you're invincible. I don't say that lightly. There's a barrier of protection around you, formed by your obedience to stay in the center of your assignment, and the enemy can't touch you. Stay in your lane, know your identity, stand on the Word meant for you, and walk in your purpose.

When you stay focused on your God-given assignment, the glory of God will be evident in your life. It may not come in the form of the largest ministry or the most well-known business, but the lives you impact will carry the weight of eternity, long after you're gone.

I own a book written by a man who lived hundreds of years ago, and yet, long after his death, people are still being blessed by his teachings. His influence endures, not because of fleeting fame, but because of the profound spiritual depth he carried.

So, which is truly better? Momentary recognition or lasting impact? Choose to do what God has called you to do, even if it doesn't appear glamorous. It may not make headlines, but it will reach further and endure longer than you could ever imagine. God knows exactly what He's doing, so trust Him, even when it feels like the excitement is happening somewhere else.

Let me pray for you:

"Father, let this truth take deep root in the hearts of Your people, so they may fully embrace Your portion, Your timing, and Your way. Even when the path doesn't align with our own desires, we trust that it leads to true life, deep spiritual growth, and the fullness of Your presence.

"In the precious name of Jesus, we pray. Amen."

Chapter Twenty-Three

The Rule of Three: A Divine Path to Glory

The passage from John 11, which recounts the raising of Lazarus from the dead, is an incredibly thought-provoking narrative. Many readers, however, rush to the climactic moment where Jesus raises Lazarus, captivated by the power of this miracle. Yet, while that moment is undeniably profound, there is immense richness in the events leading up to it—golden truths that, if we take the time to pause and reflect, can profoundly transform our approach to prayer and faith.

Jesus had already revealed to His disciples that Lazarus's sickness would not end in death, but rather it would be an opportunity for God's glory to be displayed. However, by the time He arrives, Lazarus has been in the tomb for four days. Naturally, the focus shifts to the drama of Lazarus's resurrection, but I want us to linger a bit on what happens before Jesus calls Lazarus forth.

You see, if we don't take the time to consider the *rule of three* that is subtly presented in this chapter, we might miss out on a key principle that could change how we experience the miraculous in our own lives.

Now, let's take a closer look at John 11, starting at verse 14:

> Then Jesus said to them plainly, "Lazarus is dead. And I am glad for your sakes that I was not there, that you may believe. Nevertheless let us go to him."
> Then Thomas, who is called the Twin, said to his fellow disciples, "Let us also go, that we may die with Him."
>
> —John 11:14-16

Isn't it interesting how Thomas, who is later known for his doubts, displays here a sense of reluctant acceptance rather than faith? You can almost feel the tension and confusion among the disciples. They're following Jesus, but they don't fully grasp what He's doing.

> Then Martha, as soon as she heard that Jesus was coming, went and met Him, but Mary was sitting in the house. Now Martha said to Jesus, "Lord, if You had been here, my brother would not have died. But even now I know that whatever You ask of God, God will give You."
>
> —John 11:20-22

Martha's response is a mixture of faith and resignation. She acknowledges Jesus's power but seems to have already accepted her brother's death as final. Martha believes in Jesus but struggles with understanding the fullness of His power. Jesus's response to her is crucial:

Jesus said to her, *"Your brother will rise again."* Martha said to Him, *"I know that he will rise again in the resurrection at the last day"* (John 11:23-24).

Martha's mind is on the distant future, but Jesus is about to bring that future hope into the present. He's not just talking about a distant resurrection—He's about to demonstrate that He is the resurrection and the life right now.

Jesus said to her, "I am the resurrection and the life. He who believes in Me, though he may die, he shall live. And whoever lives and believes in Me shall never die. Do you believe this?" (John 11:25-26).

This question is the heart of the matter. Jesus is challenging Martha to shift from a theoretical belief in His power to a personal, present-tense faith. This is where the rule of three comes into play, as we see in the following verses.

When Mary joins the scene, she repeats Martha's earlier sentiment: *"Then when Mary came where Jesus was and saw Him, she fell down at His feet, saying to Him, 'Lord, if You had been here, my brother would not have died'"* (John 11:32).

Both sisters express a similar faith, but it's a faith rooted in what could have been—*if only* faith. Jesus, however, is guiding them toward *now* faith.

God often prepares us for the miraculous by engaging us in a three-fold process—a process of belief, confession, and action. We see this pattern throughout Scripture, and it's present here as well.

1. **Believe:** Martha and Mary both believed in Jesus, but their belief was limited to the past and the future. Jesus calls them to believe in the present moment. When God gives you a word, it's not just for

your information—it's an invitation to believe and act on what He has said. Jesus said to Martha, *"Did I not say to you?"* Jesus point-blank reminded her of what He had previously spoken. When you're facing an impossible situation, you need a word from God that speaks directly to your circumstance. This word anchors your faith, giving you the assurance you need to move forward. It's why we pray and fast—so that we can tune our spiritual ears to hear clearly from God. Without a word from God, you're moving in the dark, and that's not where you want to be when you're seeking a miracle.

2. Declare: Jesus engages them in a confession of faith. He asks, *"Do you believe this?"* It's not enough to believe abstractly; they must verbally confess their faith in who He is right now.

What God has spoken to you must then align with your words in constant agreement. Hearing from God is one thing, but embracing that word with unwavering faith is another. When Jesus told Martha, *"If you would believe..."* He was issuing a challenge because true belief often requires going against natural evidence that might be shouting the opposite. It's easy to believe when things are going smoothly, but real faith is tested when the situation appears hopeless—just as it did with Lazarus. Believing requires you to declare that what God has spoken will come to pass.

3. Act: Here's where it all comes together. Jesus calls them to act on that belief. *"Take away the stone,"* He commands (John 11:39). This action is a demonstration of faith—it's the physical manifestation of their belief and confession. When you have fully completed all three steps, then you move into the culmination that everyone longs for. Jesus said they *"... would see the glory of God"* (John 11:40). This represents a tangible, undeniable encounter with the miraculous power of God. The glory isn't just for your benefit; it's a testimony to others of what God can do when someone dares to believe Him.

So, let's not rush to the end of the story. Let's slow down and recognize the golden principles Jesus is teaching us. The raising of Lazarus was not just a demonstration of Jesus's power over death; it was also a lesson in how we can experience the miraculous in our own lives through the rule of three.

In this passage from John 11, we find ourselves at a deeply emotional moment in the story of Lazarus. When we reach verse 35, we encounter the shortest verse in the Bible: *"Jesus wept."* It's a verse that many know by heart, but its depth and meaning are often misunderstood.

When we think of weeping, we might imagine someone overcome with emotion, shedding tears of sorrow or grief. And while there is certainly an element of deep emotion here, the original Greek word used to describe Jesus's weeping carries with it a much more complex and intense meaning. It's not just about shedding tears—it's about the deep, almost visceral response Jesus had to the situation, one that mingles sorrow with frustration and even righteous anger.

Jesus was not just mourning the death of His friend Lazarus; He was primarily confronting the thick fog of unbelief surrounding Him. He was deeply disturbed by the lack of faith in those closest to Him, who, despite all they had seen Him do, were still struggling to grasp the full extent of His true identity. A small part of His weeping was a reflection of His love for Lazarus.

Some Christians, influenced by non-biblical religious beliefs, miss the central reason Jesus wept—and it wasn't simply because Lazarus had died. This idea can be unsettling, as many cherish this brief verse with a sentimental lens, shaped by movies and dramatic portrayals. The powerful image of Jesus shedding tears over His friend's death is so ingrained that it often eclipses the greater significance of His response.

But let me ask you: if you were a Master Mechanic, renowned and at the peak of your profession, would you weep if someone brought a car to your shop with a dead battery? Would you be overwhelmed by emotion at the car's inability to start? Likely not. You'd evaluate the situation and confidently declare, "No problem—I can fix that."

Likewise, Jesus, the Master of life and death, did not weep because Lazarus had died. He knew Lazarus' death was not the end of the story. He had already declared that Lazarus would live again, and He was about to perform the miracle that would bring him back to life. Jesus wasn't surprised by Lazarus' death; in fact, He had delayed His arrival, knowing the outcome would glorify God.

So, why did Jesus weep?

Jesus wept for a much deeper, spiritual reason. He carried an agonizing burden—despite all the miracles He had performed, not one person present, not even His closest followers, truly believed or could even fathom that He was capable of raising Lazarus from the dead. Jesus wasn't weeping for Lazarus; He groaned deeply and wept because, after all the signs and wonders they had witnessed, they still did not believe.

When we move forward to the reaction of those around Jesus, we hear the murmurings: *"Could not this man, who opened the eyes of the blind, also have kept this man from dying?"* (John 11:37). They are questioning His power, just as Martha and Mary had, though in a more cynical way. It's a poignant picture of the challenges Jesus faced in His ministry—not just in performing miracles but in overcoming the entrenched unbelief that hindered people from truly experiencing God's glory.

As we continue in this story, we see that Jesus, despite the overwhelming atmosphere of unbelief, moves forward in faith. He commands the stone to be rolled away, and then, in a voice of authority, He calls Lazarus to come out. The miracle happens because He has a clear word from God to act upon, which empowers Him to confront and overcome the dense cloud of unbelief resting on the people who do not understand the ways of God.

In your own life, there will be moments when it feels like you're standing alone, battling a wave of doubt and unbelief. In those times, remember that Jesus faced similar spiritual opposition. He didn't weep out of defeat but because He bore the full weight of pushing through to victory. Jesus wept—but He also overcame.

Looking back, I can see this *rule of three* in action throughout my life and ministry. Every time I received a word from Him, believed it and acted on it, the glory showed up.

But here's the key: You can't rush this process. You can't skip steps. You must get that word from God, and once you have it, hold onto it with unwavering faith, even when everything around you challenges it.

So, if you're facing a major decision or in need of a breakthrough, step back and ask yourself: Have I received a word from God? Do I truly believe what He has told me? Am I ready to act on that word in faith? If the answer is yes, then prepare yourself—you're about to witness the glory of God in your life.

If you haven't heard from God yet, don't move forward until you do. Take the time to seek Him, fast, and pray if necessary, and get that clear directive. It's worth it because once you have it, you can move forward with confidence, knowing that you're not stepping out on your own but walking in alignment with God's perfect will for your life.

In Matthew 28, we find the Great Commission—Jesus' charge to take the gospel to all nations. While this is a universal mandate for the Church, it also calls for individual guidance from the Holy Spirit to determine where and how each of us is meant to fulfill that mission. In Acts 16, even the Apostle Paul, despite his passion for spreading the Gospel, was directed by the Holy Spirit not to preach in certain regions at specific times. This wasn't because those areas didn't need the Gospel, but because it wasn't Paul's time or assignment. This illustrates that, even as we obey the overarching commands of Scripture, we must remain attuned to the Holy Spirit's specific leading.

What we're touching on here is a profound aspect of walking in faith—a path that many admire from afar but embraced by few. It's the kind of faith that doesn't just acknowledge God's promises but relies entirely on them, without the safety nets that often hold us back from truly experiencing His glory.

Why do we sometimes feel the urge to fabricate a word or force God into giving us a certain answer? It often stems from our deep-seated desire to control our circumstances. We want things to go our way, on our terms, and in our timing. The thought of waiting, of being in a vulnerable position where we have nothing to fall back on but God, can be very uncomfortable. So instead of pressing into God—fasting, praying, and waiting for His clear direction—we might take shortcuts, creating our own path and trying to stamp God's approval on it.

But here's the reality: true faith isn't about manipulating God or our circumstances. Imagine being in a situation where you have no backup plan—no rich relative to call, no savings to dip into, no one to bail you out if things don't go as planned. All you have is a word from God. That's where the walk of faith becomes more than just a concept—it becomes your lifeline. In those moments, you find out if your faith is real, because you've got nothing else to lean on.

I've been there, and I understand the pressure. When God calls you to trust Him fully—without dropping hints to others or relying on human help—it can feel like walking a tightrope without a safety net. But it's in those moments that God shows Himself faithful. He provides in ways you never imagined, teaching you that His timing and provision are always perfect, even when they come in unexpected ways.

Yes, this path is ever upward. Jesus said, "You have to lose your life to find it." Those aren't just poetic words—they're a call to a radical way of living where you're willing to let go of your plans, your security, and your safety nets, and trust God entirely. It's raw, it's real, and sometimes it's isolating. But it's also the path that leads to God's glory being revealed in your life in ways you never thought possible.

So, if God has spoken to you—if He has given you a word—stand firmly on it. Resist the urge to seek backup plans or create safety nets in case He doesn't come through. Trust Him completely. Dare to believe what He has promised. In doing so, you'll experience your own miracle testimony, and your life will become undeniable evidence of a God who is always faithful to His word.

In conclusion, when seeking a miracle, follow the rule of three:

1. **Believe:** Seek a word from God and trust in His promise.

2. **Declare:** Speak your faith aloud with confidence.

3. **Act:** Take action and prepare to witness His glory.

By embracing these three steps, you invite God's miraculous power to work in your life.

Prayer to Give Your Heart to Jesus

If you don't know Jesus as your Lord and Savior and haven't yet made your peace with God, take a moment to do so now. Pray this prayer with me:

"Lord Jesus, I am a sinner. I want to make my life right with You. Come into my heart. Save me now. Wash away my sins and cleanse me with Your precious blood. Write my name in Your Book of Life. Jesus, step into my life, and from this day forward, lead me and guide me. In Your name, I pray. Amen."

For those who just prayed this, welcome to the family of God!

About the Author

Dr. Steven Brooks is a best-selling author, dynamic minister, and renowned teacher of God's Word, known for his operation in signs, wonders, and miracles. With a unique ability to make biblical principles clear and accessible, he reaches both new believers and those deeply rooted in faith, equipping them to walk in unwavering confidence in God's promises.

His books inspire readers to pursue a deeper relationship with God and experience the supernatural power of faith. Through his personal stories and testimonies, many have been encouraged to believe for the impossible and step into their God-given destiny. Together with his wife, Kelly, he has ministered globally, sharing the gospel with love and the power of the Holy Spirit.

As the host of *Pure Gold,* a half-hour television program reaching over 200 nations each week, Pastor Brooks brings the message of faith, hope, and transformation to audiences worldwide. His teachings extend far beyond traditional platforms—his books have been translated into multiple languages, including Russian, Mandarin,

Korean, Spanish, and Indonesian. His in-depth biblical insights are also circulated within underground churches in regions like China and Iran, where believers hunger for the truth despite persecution.

Pastor Brooks holds a doctorate in theology from Life Christian University and is a lifelong student of God's Word. Passionate about equipping believers, he provides the spiritual tools needed to live a victorious life, ablaze with God's love and power. His unwavering commitment to faith, teaching, and global outreach continues to impact lives, leading people to a closer, more transformative walk with the Lord.

www.stevenbrooks.org

Steven Brooks International
PO Box 717
Moravian Falls, NC. 28654
Email: contact@stevenbrooks.org

Steven Brooks International SPOTIFY

instagram.com/stevenbrooksint
youtube.com/stevenbrooksinternational

www.ingramcontent.com/pod-product-compliance
Lightning Source LLC
Chambersburg PA
CBHW060044100426
42742CB00014B/2689
* 9 7 8 1 6 4 4 5 7 7 9 4 3 *